THE SMALL
ROCK GARDEN

CONDITIONS OF SALE

Pan Piper Small Garden Series
Editor: C. E. Lucas Phillips

THE SMALL ROCK GARDEN

E. B. ANDERSON

A PAN ORIGINAL

PAN BOOKS LTD: LONDON

First published 1965 by
PAN BOOKS LTD
8 Headfort Place, London, S.W.1

Printed by Cox & Wyman Ltd
London, Fakenham and Reading

CONTENTS

ILLUSTRATIONS
IN PHOTOGRAVURE

LINE DRAWINGS

ACKNOWLEDGEMENTS

The photographs are my own, most of them taken in my garden, a few in the gardens of friends whose help I gratefully acknowledge. I also have to thank my sister-in-law, Sylvia Stephen, for reading the MS and pointing out where I had not made my meaning crystal clear.

FIRST THOUGHTS

IN this book the emphasis is on 'small', which means that the owner will not require outside help in making the garden, planting it or keeping it up. If the whole garden is small, as some of mine have been, lots of fun and interest will be had by making it all into a rock garden, but if you are interested in other plants you may confine yourself to one or two rock beds.

Some people talk of alpine plants, some of rock plants, and this causes some confusion. Strictly speaking, alpine plants are those that grow above where the trees end on the mountains, but for the garden we mean any dwarf plants, say, up to 9 ins. high, whether they grow in true alpine regions or near the sea-shore, whether on rocks, in stony places, in turf, in sand, or in little bogs. It really amounts to this, that it is size and hardiness which determines what we grow in our rock gardens and that the plants are perennial, for although there are many dwarf annuals it is not usual to put them in such valuable territory, for they will grow anywhere.

People often ask: what is the peculiar charm of rock plants? Well, we all grow plants for the pleasure they give us and as the result of over sixty years' experience I can say that in the small garden you will probably get more pleasure from this form of gardening than from any other. I have during my life grown most of the plants that will thrive in the open air in the British Isles, but, in what I expect to be my last garden, which is certainly small, nearly the whole of it is filled with rock plants and suitable small bulbs. Once you make acquaintance with them, especially those of a more elfin beauty, they seat themselves firmly in your heart for ever. If you doubt my word, start with one rock bed and I shall not be surprised if very soon you find you wish to make another, and another and another.

Flower Names

Some people say that they cannot stand 'those awful names', that's laziness. I beg you do not be afraid of the Latin names. Latin is everybody's language for plants, so that a Frenchman, German or Japanese will know what you mean when you mention a plant; whereas if you called a Rudbeckia, for instance, Black-eyed-Susan he would not.

All these names mean something. If you learnt Latin at school you have probably forgotten most of it, so, when you have time, say in the winter, it is worth while getting a little book explaining what the words mean. I have found the *Popular Dictionary of Botanical Names and Terms*, by G. F. Zimmer, published by Routledge & Kegan Paul, most useful.

To give an illustration, let us take the anemones. The name that comes first is the genus, in this case *Anemone*, which is derived from the Greek word anemos which means wind, hence the common name of Wind Flower; this generic name covers all anemones.

The next word in the name is that of the species, e.g. *A.narcissiflora* refers to the anemone with bunched flowers like some of the wild narcissi, *A.magellanica* is the plant that is wild near the strait of Magellan in South America, *A.nemorosa* is derived from the Latin for a grove of trees, hence the common name of Wood Anemone.

If there is a third word it will indicate that it is a variety or, as it may be called, a cultivar, e.g. *A.nemorosa flore pleno* is the variety with full or double flowers, or *A.nemorosa* Blue Bonnet, a selected blue form.

Not all are as easy as this example, by any means, and it must be admitted that our little rock plants (like dwarf conifers) are often labelled with names that seem very trying until one becomes familiar with them. Moreover, with a few exceptions, such as wallflower, candytuft, woodruff and so on, they have no vernacular names, so we have no option but to use the botanical ones.

Synonyms create another kind of difficulty, even for old

hands. The professional botanists are constantly changing the names of plants for technical reasons. Thus *Anemone pulsatilla* was re-christened *Pulsatilla vulgaris* a few years ago. Nurserymen are naturally slow to drop the familiar, older names, so, where two names are current, I try to give both in this book. It is as interesting as a cross-word puzzle finding out what the names of your plants mean. If this book persuades you to start it will have fulfilled its main purpose.

CHAPTER 2

WHERE ROCK PLANTS COME FROM

ALTHOUGH it will not enable you to grow rock plants more successfully, it should add interest to know where they come from. A few grow in our own mountains – those of Snowdonia, the Lake District, the Scottish Highlands and the Irish Mountains; for example, the moss campion (*Silene acaulis*), the purple saxifrage (*Saxifraga oppositifolia*) and the Mountain Avens (*Dryas octopetala*), but these are rare and to filch them from their native haunts for our gardens is a form of vandalism.

As one would expect, the mountains of Europe are the home of a great number of the plants we grow, such as aquilegia, campanula, dianthus, gentian, ranunculus and saxifrage and many others. These come from the mountains of Austria, the Balkans, France, Greece, Italy, Spain and Switzerland; also the Caucasus in Southern Russia.

Others, such as aethionema, arnebia, erodium, verbascum, etc., come from the countries of the Near East with their hotter summers, such as Cyprus, the Lebanon, Turkey and Iran. A few come from the Atlas mountains in North Africa, for instance anacyclus, but the remainder of this continent is too hot to provide us with hardy plants except the Drakensburg mountains of South Africa, which rise to 10,000 ft and have given us, among a few other things, the well known rhodo-hypoxis.

Many plants, such as androsace, codonopsis, cyananthus, incarvillea, meconopsis and especially primula, have come from the vast range of the Himalayas, Tibet, and the mountain masses of South West China. Going farther east, Japan has provided many good things, several aquilegias but particularly shortia and schizocodon. Travelling south, Australia is too hot, but the south island of New Zealand, with mountains running its whole length, has sent us many things which do not occur, or rarely, anywhere else, such as celmisia, ourisia, raoulia and hebe (shrubby veronicas).

Western Sources

There remains America. North America comes second to Europe in providing suitable plants, chiefly from the mountains in the West, and many grow nowhere else. From here come dodecatheon, eriogonum, lewisia, evening primrose, penstemon, phlox and zauschneria. As South America has high mountains running from north to south on the West, the Andes, one would have expected many rock plants to have come from there also, but in reality we have very few, for these mountains are very inaccessible and, being in the southern hemisphere, their seasons are the reverse of ours, so that the plants do not take easily to our summer, being their winter.

This is curious because although the same reversal of seasons applies to New Zealand, plants from there do not give us any great difficulty. However, all our hardy calceolarias come from South American mountains and the best oxalis.

Finally, the nearer we get to the Poles, the colder it is on the lower ground even down to the sea-shore, so there it is that we find many dwarf hardy plants which in other parts we are obliged to climb many thousands of feet to see. By contrast, it is in the mountains of the Near East, Iran, North Africa, Southern Greece, Spain, Portugal and California, where the summers are hot and dry, that we get most of the dwarf bulbs which are so useful in the rock garden; to mention a few, crocus, chionodoxa, iris, narcissus, scilla, tulip and brodiaea, but lack of space prevents their inclusion in this book.

Sometimes the same plant will grow on the mountains of several countries, others are confined to a particular mountain range or even a particular mountain or even a particular spot on that mountain. On some mountains there may be hundreds of the same plant, on others only a few scattered here and there

B

and one must tramp over many miles to find them. We gardeners owe a great debt to the plant collectors who, often for a very meagre reward, have, without exaggeration, risked their lives to send home the plants or seeds which have made our gardens the richest in the world. We also owe many good plants to those who wander in the more accessible places, sometimes definitely looking for plants, sometimes finding a gem by accident, and these finds gradually get into the gardens of those who love them and then into the nurseries. Most gardeners are friendly and generous people, so you will get a lot of fun out of meeting other rock gardeners as well as growing the plants.

CHAPTER 3

ROCK PLANTS IN THE WILD

WITH increased leisure and ease of travel, it is to be hoped that those of you who are interested in growing rock plants will take the opportunity of seeing some of them on the mountains, for no description can equal what will be learnt by a fortnight among the plants as they grow there. For those who for one reason or another cannot do so, this short description of the conditions under which rock plants live is given so that the reason for the chapters which follow will be better understood.

In these regions and altitudes the winters are long with much snow, lasting from about October or November to June, but when spring comes at last the change is very rapid, the snow melts in the hot sun and, as soon as the earth is exposed, the plants which have been asleep all the winter wake up and many, such as soldanella and crocus, come into flower a few feet from where the snow lies. Although in the mountains in the winter the air temperature is very low, with many degrees of frost, the snow blanket prevents the soil becoming anything like as cold, so the plants are not killed but simply remain at rest.

In this country winter frosts can be damaging even to mountain plants, because we seldom get the snow cover and as a result the plants suffer lower temperatures than they do in the wild. Moreover, our alternation of periods of cold and warmth are damaging, because the latter may cause growth to start and then a subsequent frost is particularly killing. The dwarf form of many of the plants is nature's method of preserving the plant from injury, not only by the great weight of snow under which it lies during the winter but also as a protection against the blizzards, storms of rain and fierce gales which may occur before or after the snow cover has formed.

Protection from Drought

The intense ultra-violet light which causes the burning of our skin in such places and the lavish use of lotions plays its part in keeping the plant compact. In places where the summers are particularly hot and dry, to prevent death from drought the plants not only adopt a cushion-like form, which offers the smallest surface to the sun and wind, but have the added protection of silver hairs, thin spiny or wax-covered leaves, or else fat leaves which store water for use in difficult times, such as in the sedums and house-leeks.

As well as the visible stems and leaves all plants have roots to provide them with water and the chemicals necessary for their life, and the conditions under which these develop are very different from those of most lowland plants. Starting high up sometimes they are in rock crevices so narrow that it is difficult to insert even the point of a knife, but in such the roots will extend for several feet in search of the little moisture that percolates the crack and the food from the traces of vegetable debris that wash in. It is a very spartan life indeed, possibly helped by some moisture absorbed by the leaves. These 'crevice plants' are among the most difficult to cultivate.

Other mountain plants grow on layers of rock where an inch or two of soil has accumulated over many years from the decay of lichens and mosses and the dead leaves of the plants which follow these, mixed with fragments of rock, and the roots of these plants may likewise wander into crevices in the rock ledge.

Beneath the rocks with crevices and ledges we find sloping banks of very stony soil, lots of stones, small and large, and in the lower layers grit and sand and not much soil, but with snow water percolating beneath for part of the year. These are the 'screes' and in them grow many of the plants which are most valuable in the rock garden. In places with really hot and dry summers, where the supply of winter snow or rain water soon fails, the plants make up for this by developing very long roots which are able to go down through the stones and soil to parts which never become dust-dry.

Below the screes, from the accumulation and decomposition of dead plants and the grinding down of the rocks by rain and frost, the ground, although still full of stones of all sizes, contains much more soil and, as would be expected, a greater number of plants and on the whole the plants which are the easiest to grow.

Farther down still, where there is still more soil, we come to the meadows, which provide what we commonly call herbaceous plants.

With all the stone present as indicated above it is obvious that the ground is always well drained, even though it may be well watered, and this drainage is a fundamental thing in successful rock plant cultivation.

Another point that is sometimes overlooked is that in the high mountains plants are not necessarily in full sun all day, for the high peaks which usually remain snow-covered throw shadow at one period or another. It is only on south-facing rocks and extensive flat areas, such as the meadows or low flat-topped hills, that the plants are in sun from morning until night, and then banks, ridges and gullies will provide shade for those requiring it.

Some of the plants we grow come from the woods, mostly of pines or firs, which clothe the sides of many mountains. The soil will still be full of stones but these will be mixed mainly with leaf-mould and sand washed from higher up. The difference is that the plants are in full shade almost all the day and every year they get a top dressing of dead leaves.

CHAPTER 4

MAKING THE SMALL ROCK GARDEN

ASPECT – SLOPES – DRAINAGE – ACIDITY – PLACING THE STONES

THE first consideration is where the rock garden is to be placed or, as I recommend, the *first* rock bed. By starting with one bed, apart from the cost of materials, you will learn by experience which plants succeed best in the soil (suitably modified if necessary) and climate of your garden. Following this, additional beds may be made which, when completed, will in effect make a rock garden. One of the most successful growers I knew proceeded in this way and in any one year confined himself to the construction of one bed, although cost was not a consideration. Now, where shall we put this bed?

Aspect

It should be in an open part of the garden, not near enough to trees or hedges, if any, for their roots to wander into it, and rob the soil of moisture and food. It does not matter if distant trees or buildings throw shade for not more than half of the day. In the northern counties and Scotland and places where there is a lot of rain, like parts of Wales and the South West, the bed should run from east to west, with the main slope to the south, so that it gets all the sun possible.

In drier areas such as the South and East, the bed may run north and south, so that all the plants do not receive full sun all the day; those on the top obviously will but not those at the sides.

Although rock plants do not mind a reasonable amount of wind, like ourselves, they do object to draughts such as occur in and near the narrow spaces between houses, and they object very much to the drying east winds when growth is commencing in the spring; so walk about the garden when this wind is blowing before choosing the site. A hedge planted on the east side some distance away, say on the far side of a path, to avoid its roots growing into the bed, makes a good break, as does trellis work, which can be used for climbing plants.

Slopes

This advice refers to gardens which are flat or nearly so; if on a sharp slope, the aspect is already determined for you, but it will not prevent success provided suitable plants are chosen. There are two alternatives for such a position: either to put rocks in the slope as it exists, when it should look like a bit of mountain-side, or to cut out terraces about 1 ft high and 18 ins. wide, the soil of which will be held up by stones built up like a low wall.

If the slope faces south these terraces will be ideal for sun lovers; if it faces north the same procedures may be used and many plants which dislike full scorching sun will be happier there than anywhere else. A narrow path 15 to 18 ins. wide should be made at the bottom of each terrace. If the slope is not terraced, a similar path should run so that any part of the planted part can be reached without walking on the plants, which means that the beds should be at the widest not more than 6 ft across between the paths.

One of the most important things in growing rock plants successfully is the soil and, because of expense, it is desirable to use as much of the natural soil as possible. In a level garden the rock beds must be above the ground level and the best way to obtain the necessary soil is to excavate it from where the paths are to be, and make these up with ashes and broken bricks and any similar material and top them with gravel or stone chips. The soil thus obtained free of charge, with any other available, is made into an irregular mound which can be about 1-1½ ft high for every 5 ft in width and I find that beds 5-6 ft across at the widest part are the most convenient for the

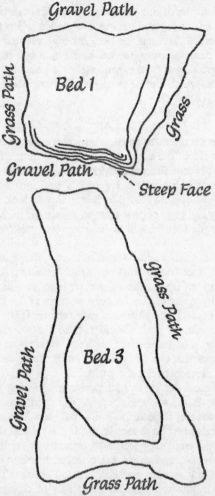

FIGS. 1 & 2. Ground Plans of Rock Beds.

The lines indicate ridges of rocks; the closer they are together
the steeper the slope. Where there are no additional lines the
bed slopes down to the stones at the edge.

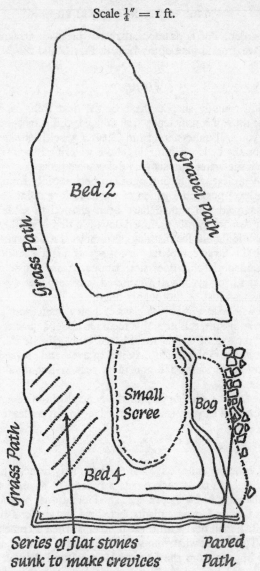

Scale ¼″ = 1 ft.

Bed 2

Gravel Path

Grass Path

Small Scree

Bog

Grass Path

Bed 4

Series of flat stones
sunk to make crevices

Paved
Path

These four beds and the paths (including the broad central one) are contained in an area of 530 sq. ft.

small garden. For appearance they can be made irregular in shape (see ground plan of my beds in Figs. 1 and 2).

Drainage

Having roughly shaped the bed, the next thing is to test whether the soil is sufficiently well drained; this is most important, as you will understand from Chapter 3, so that water does not lie on the beds when it rains and if watering is necessary in droughts the water quickly gets down to the roots.

The simplest way to find out is to pour rapidly from a can on to a level position a gallon of water. Before doing this the freshly moved soil should have been allowed to settle for a week or two and gently trampled down, so that it will be in the condition it should for planting, also moist but not wet. If the water drains away completely in 10–15 seconds it is sufficiently well drained. If this does not happen, stone chips, gravel, coarse sand, or even well-weathered, coarse boiler (not fire-grate) ashes must be thoroughly dug in.

This will be essential with clays or heavy loams and, as well as these additions, it is desirable to mix in about a quarter of the bulk of moss-peat or leaf-mould, and test again. If the water runs away too rapidly, as it may with gravels and coarse sands, then add some loamy soil and moss-peat or leaf-mould, and test again.

If the soil is a sandy peat, for the general run of rock plants the addition of a loamy soil is essential, even if it passes the test.

Acidity

Soils, whether sand, clay, loam or peat, may be acid, neutral or alkaline. For most rock plants a neutral or alkaline (limy) soil is the best, but some, such as rhododendrons, Asiatic gentians and many Japanese plants, hate lime and prefer a slightly acid soil. I shall deal with these problems when I come to the plants. To find out what your soil reaction, as it is called, is, it is best to inquire from the County Horticultural Adviser, who should know the soil of the district. This will avoid waste of money and disappointment from buying plants that are not suitable for your soil, and may die almost at the look of it.

Placing the Stones

Although rock plants may be grown on the mound prepared as described without any rocks at all, few gardeners would wish to do so and it is always desirable to have a few stones to raise the edges of the mound at least 4 ins. above path level, where nasty cold and damp air settles in the winter. Apart from this, many plants like being against a stone, as the soil is always moister there.

Obviously it is most economical to use local stone and, even if not beautiful, like weathered limestone, it will not look out of place, as limestone often does. Mixed sizes are desirable, with the biggest not more than 56 lb. in weight, so that you can handle them without slipping a disc.

The placing will depend on your taste, but every stone should be buried at least half its depth in the soil with the broadest face in the ground and the soil well rammed round it so that, when in position, it is possible to stand upon it without it rocking. This is very important if a big-footed friend tries to get a closer look at something! Some of the stones may be buried deeper so that only a small portion shows above ground. The sketches in Fig. 3 will show you what I mean. All soil should slope gently towards the stones edging the bed. On a natural slope this problem does not arise.

Where stones are placed next to each other they must be as close as possible, to prevent the soil washing through the space. If a space is unavoidable then a smaller stone must be rammed in to fill it. On the north-facing side the mound may be at its highest and the soil held up by stones placed on the top of each other, but each one about 1 in. back from the stone below and a thin layer of rotted turf placed between each as mortar. This will give positions for such shade lovers as haberlea and ramonda, which dislike being planted on the flat.

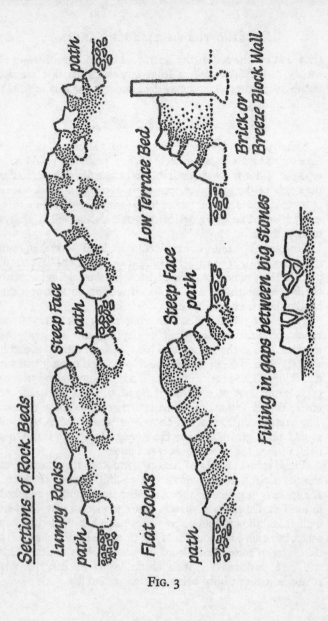

Sections of Rock Beds

Lumpy Rocks

path

Steep Face
path

Flat Rocks

path

Steep Face
path

Low Terrace Bed

Brick or
Breeze Block Wall

Filling in gaps between big stones

FIG. 3

If possible, visit a small rock garden in the neighbourhood and see how the stones are placed as it is much easier to learn from an example than it is from any description in words, even combined with sketches.

CHAPTER 5

OTHER WAYS OF GROWING ROCK PLANTS

PAVEMENTS – DRY WALLS – PEAT WALLS – SLEEPER BEDS – SCREES –
ASH AND BRICK BEDS – MOIST BEDS

THE rock bed as described in the previous chapter is not the only means of growing rock plants, even if the most satisfactory as a picture; further, some plants may do better in the conditions existing in one or other of the schemes about to be described which, if there is room, can be a useful and interesting addition to the rock bed itself.

Pavements

In some places irregular rocks may be unobtainable, but flat stones such as those from broken pavements may be available. Even if of concrete, this may be used and the glaring whiteness toned down by painting with a solution of sulphate of iron at the rate of 2 oz. per gallon of water.

The soil should be prepared and tested as for a rock bed, and the bed edged with old bricks or stones of similar shape. The soil should slope down to the edge, so that at the back it is about 1 in. higher for every foot width; this is to prevent water lying in it. I have such a bed 3 ft wide, a useful width, and the back is 4 ins. higher than the front. This bed, incidentally, is 20 ft long and contains over 150 plants.

The flat stones are then placed on the soil with gaps of about ¾ in. between them. Take a good walk all over the bed and if any stones sink much below the others, lift and put some more soil underneath. When the surface is approximately level, fill in the spaces between the stones with the same soil as underneath, but with a quarter of its bulk of coarse sand added. Many plants like the conditions thus provided – a cool root-run under the stones, and the foliage out of contact with damp earth and free from soil spatter in rain.

Dry Walls

Many plants like the vertical positions provided by dry walls, where there is no danger of moisture hanging round their necks, but such walls do require an astonishing amount of stone. They may be built against a bank or other wall, not the house walls! Or they may form the boundaries of a raised bed of any length and width.

For satisfactory construction, roughly rectangular stones are essential, such as may be seen in many parts of the country where dry walls are used for boundaries. The kind of stone does not matter. If the height desired is not more than 2 ft, the stones may be laid one on the top of another, as building with bricks.

It is a counsel of perfection which I have never been able to follow to put in the plants as the wall is built; if you are able to do this put a little soil, preferably heavy soil, on the stone, spread out the roots, put a little more soil over them and then the next stone. If planting is not possible until the wall is complete, place as 'mortar' a ½-in. layer of rotted turf or heavy soil between the stones. When planting, which should in these circumstances be done only in the autumn, a hole is gouged out with a very narrow trowel or piece of steel bent into a U like a potato peeler. Use small plants, spread their roots out, teasing them in as far as possible with a wedge-shaped bit of wood, squirt in a little water, and plug the hole with a bit of turf or heavy soil and a fragment of stone rammed in to finish off.

If the dry walls are used to make rectangular or irregular raised beds, then 2 ft high is enough, but the width must be not less than 1 ft, or as much more as you like. Fill the hollow interior with soil as prepared for rock beds and tread it down well as construction proceeds. Plants may be grown in the sides and on the top, and many like being raised well above ground level; also the perfect drainage which means no stagnant moisture. Such beds may be seen at Kew and in the Savill Gardens at Windsor.

Peat Walls

If one lives in a district where blocks of peat are readily available it is possible to use these instead of stone for low retaining walls, but if the only peat blocks obtainable are those used as fuel the wall cannot safely be more than 15 ins. high and before use the blocks must be thoroughly soaked in water, then laid like bricks, i.e. no joints directly above one another, and pressed well together. I am satisfied that these walls of small blocks are only satisfactory in districts where there is a fairly heavy rainfall, say 30–35 ins. a year, and for beds in, at least, partial shade, or in a cool climate such as in Scotland, or if one is prepared to water frequently. Many plants, such as the Asiatic gentians, ourisias and various ericaceous plants, certainly like these blocks and run into them, often in preference to the attractive soil mixture behind.

Sleeper Beds

Another system to make low raised beds without stone is to use old railway sleepers, of which plenty should be available these days! One sleeper on edge gives a height of 10 ins. and they should be held in position by short iron rods $1\frac{1}{2}$ ft long, bent over about 1 in. at the top and flattened, and pointed at the other end, driven into the ground close to the sleepers with the flattened end gripping the topmost sleeper.

Any soil mixture desired can be filled into the rectangular bed so formed, including a special mixture of one third sand, one third moss-peat, one third non-limy loam or leaf-mould for lime haters, if you are on lime. Such a bed may be placed in sun or shade according to the plants it is desired to grow. I have seen some very happy plants in such beds.

Screes

Probably the cheapest and easiest method of growing rock plants other than shade or moisture lovers is to use screes. Most gardeners make these to contain the more difficult plants, but often the easy ones do even better than in other places; the two should not be planted in the same scree bed, however, otherwise the easy will swamp the difficult.

Experts differ much about the best depth for a scree and also on the mixture to be used, which, you will understand from Chapter 3, will consist very largely of broken stone and grit. I think the depth depends on what your natural soil is about a foot down; if heavy clay, then 18 ins. is desirable, if sand or gravel or sandy loam, 12 ins. is sufficient.

The soil blend best suited to a scree in most districts is the 50/50 mixture. First take say 50 parts of washed $\frac{1}{4}$–$\frac{1}{2}$ in. gravel, limestone chips, granite chips or any broken rock of the same size which is not so soft that it breaks down into sand or dust when weathered. Then mix this well with 50 per cent of a mixture of equal parts of loam and moss peat. If you cannot obtain loam use John Innes Seed Compost.

Having dug the hole to any shape you like, fill in the bottom of the 18-in. hole with broken brick, stones, pieces of rock or even clinker; on this spread pieces of old sacking to prevent the scree mixture from falling into this special drainage. Then fill up either the 18-in. or 12-in. hole with the mixture given to ground level.

Make the scree an inch or two higher in some places and, if you have a few rocks available, bury these almost to the top, both for effect and to make stepping stones. If your soil is heavy clay it is desirable to raise the whole scree 3–4 ins. above ground level by means of edging stones.

The aspect may be the same as for rock beds and, as watering is very easy, it does not matter whether the scree is in sun or half shade, although the latter is better in hot, dry areas. In areas of heavy rainfall it may be an advantage to replace say $\frac{1}{10}$th of the loam with coarse sand.

The test of a satisfactory scree is that water poured upon it runs through it at once. The ultimate test will be how the plants thrive, so make a small one for a start and for additions alter the mixture up or down as regards the stone, so to speak, according to what you find necessary, if any alteration is indicated. It will be obvious that for lime haters limestone chips should not be used.

Ash and Brick Beds

Ash beds are really screes made of boiler ashes instead of chips or gravel and are most economical in cost and in my experience equally successful, but one must use the correct type of ash. This is ash from factory boilers which will not pass through an $\frac{1}{8}$-in. sieve; that is to say from which all dust has been removed and from which also large clinkers should be picked out.

Further, such ash is not safe to use until it has been weathered for about six months; left to lie in the open and watered and turned at intervals like a compost heap it will then be fit to use exactly as described for chippings, etc. The appearance will be like the ashes round a volcano.

Another alternative sometimes available is crushed red brick, not the hard blue. This only needs sieving, but the appearance of such a scree is rather lurid and the colour does not blend with all flowers.

Moist Beds

There are many choice dwarf woodland plants and others native to damp places that the rock gardener is likely to wish to grow, so if there is no naturally damp place in the garden it is necessary to make one. The position should be in as full shade as possible, but not near enough to trees for their roots to penetrate; shade on the north side of the house or other buildings or walls is ideal.

Excavate the garden soil to a depth of 1 ft and fill in the hole to ground level, or just below, with a mixture of $\frac{1}{4}$ loam, $\frac{1}{4}$ moss-peat, $\frac{1}{4}$ leaf-mould, $\frac{1}{4}$ sand; if the surrounding soil is clay or a heavy loam the bed will remain moist with an occasional watering. It is possible that the addition of the peat and sand forked in to 1 ft will make such heavy soil porous enough but still moisture-retaining and so will save buying loam or leaf-mould.

If sand or gravel, it is a good dodge to line the hole with black polythene, tucking the edges in 2–3 ins. below the surrounding soil and then filling in with the mixture. At the lowest point cut a hole about 2 ins. diameter to allow surplus water to drain away, as this is not supposed to be a bog. If a miniature bog is what you want, however, the drainage hole should be omitted, as surplus water will soak away over the edges.

The idea of all these odds and ends of beds is to help you to grow as many different kinds of plants as you feel inclined and also to give you a chance with those which for one reason or other are not happy in your ordinary rock garden. Besides, if you have more than one plant of anything, it is wise to try them in one of these special beds; the plant cannot tell you before-hand where it would like to be. There would be an awful noise in some gardens if they could.

CHAPTER 6

CULTIVATION OF ROCK PLANTS

ON BUYING PLANTS – PLANTING – WEEDING – WATERING –
FEEDING AND TOP DRESSING – LABELLING – ARRANGEMENT OF
PLANTS – TRIAL AND ERROR

BEFORE dealing with planting, the methods of cultivation and
care of the plants, a few words on buying plants may be
useful.

If there is a nursery near at hand which sells even a limited
selection of rock plants then go there first, as you can pick
out plants of reasonable size and also save the cost of packing
and carriage, which may be considerable. Moreover, a local
nursery is most likely to grow plants suitable for the district.

For some plants you may have to deal with nurseries too far
away to visit, except perhaps on holiday; if so deal only with
nurseries of repute (many of which are listed at the end of this
book) or which may be recommended by other rock gardeners.
Probably the best way to obtain information is to join the
Alpine Garden Society or the Scottish Rock Garden Club, or
both, very cheap at £1 a year, as advertisers in these journals
can be depended upon and their members will always be ready
with advice.

Do not be tempted by 'cheap lots', for a good-sized plant
takes time and skill to produce and is therefore worth the price
asked. On the other hand, at times, unjustifiably small plants
are sent out, even by good nurseries, which really need nursing
in a pot for a year, which the beginner cannot be expected to do.

Therefore, until you become wise about the quality of the
plants supplied, it is advisable to put on your order 'Do not
send any plants which are not of reasonable size'. Reasonable
size depends on how big the plant will eventually become, e.g.

an aubrieta should not be less than 2½–3 ins. across, an aretian 'bun' androsace cannot be expected to be more than 1 in. An obviously young seedling or recently rooted cutting should not be accepted. Until you have experience with a fairly large collection of the easier plants do not be led astray by alluring advertisements of 'novelties', which may be here today and gone tomorrow.

Examine the packing and if it is such that the soil has been shaken away from the plants or some plants are lying about loose, do not hesitate to complain.

Order early when you get a catalogue so that you may receive the plants at a suitable planting time, but realize that no nurseryman can promise to deliver plants on a particular date, as weather may upset all his plans.

Do not be disappointed if the nurseryman cannot supply all your order; it is difficult for him to calculate demand and weather or other hazards may reduce his stocks. But if you have sent for and receive a catalogue without charge, it is only fair to do your best to send an order, for catalogues nowadays cost much and the nurseryman must live.

Planting

Having ordered and received or begged your plants, the first question is when to plant? This to a certain extent will depend on convenience, but within limits there are good and not so good times when to plant. In dry districts and those likely to be so in spring and early summer and where the summer may be hot, and where the surrounding soil is of a dry nature such as gravels or sands, without doubt the best time is September or October, so that the plants may become established before winter comes on.

Where the rainfall is high or the soil and air of the district likely to be damp, such as on the clays and heavy loams, March to April are the better months, as the plants are not then subjected to cold, damp soil and air before they have re-rooted. The disadvantage of spring planting is that at this period we often experience a period of cold drying east or north-east winds. This means that water must be given until the plants are established and begin to grow. The alternative, and better, system is to 'puddle' them in. This means that, before putting in the plant, the hole is filled with water and the plant inserted as soon as this has drained away.

That famous gardener, the late E. A. Bowles, used to say that one could plant any time when the ground was not frozen. This, in a sense, is true; it means in summer 'puddling' and providing shade for a time until growth starts and in winter giving the protection of a cloche or piece of glass until the spring comes, which keeps the soil warmer, prevents constant beating by the rain and keeps off a certain amount of frost.

The exception to the above advice is that the planting of rock walls should always be done in September or October, as sufficient watering of these in a dry spring is almost impossible. Likewise in screes or ash beds, because of the rapid drainage, I prefer autumn planting unless one is prepared to attend regularly to watering if the weather is dry.

When the plants arrive remove weeds, if any, and the drainage material from the bottom of the ball of soil unless this has been shaken free, as it often is during transit. Make the hole wide enough to take the full width of the roots and deep enough so that the longest roots go straight down to the bottom; do not twist the roots to get them in. By holding the plant upright in the left hand, allowing the roots to hang down, the depth of hole required is easily judged.

Sometimes it will be found that the roots are twisted round in the ball of soil as the result of pot culture, the usual system of growing rock plants for sale. If this is so, allow the soil to dry sufficiently so that, when the ball is tapped, it falls away and frees the roots; this is better than putting the tight ball of soil straight into the hole, as the old roots never become untwisted.

Position the plant so that the top is just level with the surface of the bed, fill in the soil to the level and press gently with the back of the trowel or with the thumb; the soil should be firm but not hard rammed. A surfacing of chips or coarse sand round the plant gives a good finish.

In planting the scree or ash bed, which should be moist or the stones will keep slipping into the hole, one needs only to fill in with the mixture, without pressing down, as too much pressure or ramming may cause the rough scree material to damage the roots.

There remain dry walls when planting has not been done during erection. For these the soil must be gently shaken from the roots when the ball is sufficiently dry and the hole made with a U trowel as already described. Before inserting and teasing in the roots, I syringe water into the hole so that the soil is thoroughly wetted before the plant is inserted. The hole should then be filled with bits of rotted turf or a heavy loam, particular care being taken to see that this is pushed to the bottom of the hole with a small wooden wedge, the plant and its roots being placed against one side. Small plants are essential, as working in the roots of a large plant is virtually impossible unless the crevice is larger than is desirable, for soil easily washes out of large crevices.

Weeding

Rock plants should always be kept free from weeds, for, apart from taking up some of the food, they can easily smother the smaller plants and, by keeping their foliage wet, injure their health even if they do not kill them. Particularly objectionable are 'poppers', or bitter cress, which shoot their seeds all over the place; they and groundsel and one or other of the grasses are the commonest and easiest to remove, but dandelions need a narrow trowel to get to the end of the roots unless very young, also any of the thistles. If one of these tap-rooted weeds appears in the middle of a plant it is impossible to use a trowel without damaging the plant itself; the only thing to do is to pick off the leaves constantly, when it will become so weakened that it will die or can be pulled out with finger and thumb.

Pearl-wort, which makes moss-like tufts, is another nuisance and seeds about profusely; it has extraordinarily tenacious roots and requires loosening with, say, a two-pronged fork. The small seedlings are difficult to pull out, so I cut through them with a knife run just under the surface of the soil. These, with groundsel, are my weeds, yours may be different and you must learn how to deal with them.

Watering

Rock plants require water for their annual growth but the amount required varies much – from the little required by plants from arid regions, where quickly melting snow or an occasional shower gives sufficient, to those that receive water from the melting snow of the high peaks as well as rain during most of their growing period, until they begin to ripen seed, or those that are in a constantly moist position.

In our climate any of these plants may receive water at any time during the year, whether they want it or not, but the usual thing here is to be short of water in the growing period of spring and early summer. Some people water regularly during this period if the weather is dry, but I prefer plants to work for themselves as far as possible by getting their roots deeper down where the soil is always moist and I water only if plants in the rock beds and pavement show signs of flagging; this may be only an excuse for laziness. Shade plants do receive water and also the scree.

Writing this in June 1964, the rock beds and pavement have had no artificial watering this season, but then I live at 400 ft and in the cool Cotswolds. I suggest water if you must, and then give a *good* watering; if your beds are made as suggested you can pour the water on from the spout of the can, and then refrain until it again becomes really necessary.

Feeding and Top Dressing

Although the majority of rock plants do not require rich food, it is obvious that, if they are making satisfactory growth, they will be continually taking up food from the soil and probably more than they do in their native homes, because there they get a definite period of rest, whereas here they seldom get a real rest with mild winter weather alternating with cold – a life of grow and stop, stop and grow.

To make up for this I believe in regular feeding, so that there is food at hand in the larder whenever required, and I think this is a better practice than the remaking often recommended, which means re-soiling the rock garden every so many years, for this is a laborious and expensive job, entailing the removal of all the plants. Therefore every winter I give the beds a dusting of a mixture of bonemeal and sulphate of potash. 14 oz. of the former and 2 oz. of the latter. Sufficient is given to make the beds look as if they had been dusted with flour; this soon washes in and a month or two later no visible trace will be left.

Sometimes as a change I dress with a mixture of 3 parts of bonemeal and one of Maxicrop powder to supply any trace elements that may be missing, but I have no proof that this is superior.

Someone may say, what about beds containing lime haters, such as rhododendrons and other ericaceous plants (since bonemeal has an alkaline reaction)? I have known in one famous garden rhododendrons fed with bonemeal without ill effect, but if you are fortunate enough to have supplies of non-limy leaf-mould then use this preferably for such things. If you are frightened by the idea of bonemeal, give a dusting of hoof-and-horn. In both the idea is that the food in bonemeal and hoof-and-horn is only slowly released for the plants' use. All the plants we are dealing with dislike, or rather make too much growth, if quick-acting artificial fertilisers are used, and become too sappy to withstand our usual weather conditions.

Plants growing in the shade normally enjoy a somewhat richer diet and for the shade beds I use, on my limy soil and in the absence of leaf-mould, 5 parts of moss-peat, 1 part of Maxicrop powder, which provide humus, and about $\frac{1}{4}$–$\frac{1}{2}$ part of dried blood, to give the little extra that woodland plants like.

Those fortunate enough to have plenty of leaf-mould may substitute this for the moss-peat and the same mixture may be applied on acid soils.

In the mountains fresh grit, sand and some humus are washed down among the plants by rain and snow water and when the snow melts plants will often be found almost buried in a new layer of gritty soil. This is nature's way of feeding and top-dressing at the same time, or perhaps one should say that is what happens and the plants have to 'lump' it whether they like it or not; they seem to like it.

In the garden the soil gradually sinks and some may wash to the lower level, leaving plants higher out of the ground than is desirable, and tufted plants hollow in the middle. To compensate for this a top dressing of the beds and the screes in the spring is desirable, which top dressing should be dry enough to be worked into tufted plants like drabas, saxifragas, pinks, etc., with the fingers. I use old potting soil, of which I generally have plenty, as I raise many plants from seed and the mixture I use is sufficiently gritty for the purpose. If this is not available, use John Innes Seed Compost 2 parts with 1 part coarse sand or fine grit thoroughly mixed. Of course, apply when the plants are dry, otherwise the dressing will stick to the wet foliage.

Labelling

When the collection is small it is very easy to think that one will remember the name of every plant put in; you may, particularly if you grow only wild species, but if you grow a number of garden varieties it is sometimes rather difficult to remember whether a certain plant is Dainty Maid or Angelina Buggins.

Labelling therefore is important and the problem certainly is what label to use – one which is not too large for small plants, on which the writing will remain visible for several years and which, when in a jolly mood, the blackbirds cannot scatter all over the place. Further they should not be expensive. Stamped lead labels are all very well but the machine for doing the stamping is expensive and the process tedious.

I now use Hartley Shrub labels which have a long stem, not the pointed ones the removal of which by the birds is child's play. I always recommend these when lecturing and why Hartley's do not push them is a mystery to me. So often I meet people who have tried to get them and cannot from the ordinary suppliers of garden needs.

For writing on them I use a soft lead or wax pencil but this remains legible for only 2–3 years, depending on the exposure. An indelible ink lasts longer, but I have never found the writing with this really permanent, say over ten years. If a weather-proof varnish could be found to cover the writing on these labels then I think for the small garden the problem would be solved.*

Plastic labels can be used with the pencil but this is no more permanent than on the Hartley. I see that now an acid indelible ink is advertised; this should eat into the plastic and, even if it fades, as eventually I am sure it will, it may have etched the label and such etching is easy to read if the label is held at the right angle to the light. Of course, varnishing again would be an advantage.

Arrangement of Plants

To avoid future trouble, it is essential before planting to know how the plants grow, whether as mats, small or wide bushlets or as mounds or buns. In the chapters on the plants themselves I shall as far as possible endeavour to indicate the habit, so all that is necessary here is to advise planting the mat-formers and wide bushlets in the lower parts of the beds and the buns and little tufts and small bushlets higher up, thus one type will not smother the other. Or use one bed for the bigger things and one for the smaller.

Another bit of advice: the spreaders and large bushlets will benefit from cutting them back soon after flowering, it will

* I have one under test now.

keep them neat and compact and avoid their wasting their energy on seed production. This refers to such plants as some alyssums, aubrieta, arabis, some pinks, hebes, iberis, shrubby penstemons, etc.; they will then make compact new growth ready for the next season.

Trial and Error

Now before we come to the plants themselves a few words of what I hope is wisdom. Even if you follow my advice I cannot guarantee you a hundred per cent success; I do not reach this myself after over sixty years, and, having grown at some time or other nearly every plant I shall mention, I doubt if any others do. This, of course, refers to outdoor rock gardening, which is my subject.

Every garden differs from another, even different parts of the same garden. Your neighbour over the fence may grow mats of some plant that with you remain at 2–3 ins. across, but you may have healthy specimens of plants that he cannot grow at all. You do not know why, he does not know why, nor do I. All I am able to do is to give you suggestions which should lead to reasonable success. I cannot give you Mrs Beeton-type recipes which will always result in a vigorous and happy plant.

I have been in my present garden four years and it is on a stony, heavy, limy loam, in a valley, which I have never experienced previously. I lose plants and shall probably continue to lose plants until I understand the conditions thoroughly, and cease to try those which are impossible in this particular site.

You will, unless remarkably lucky, do the same, but in the course of years, as you learn the peculiarities of the garden and also which groups of plants like you, you should be able to build up a collection of happy plants which will be a delight to yourself, and your friends. If a plant looks unhappy do not hesitate to move it to another position any time except in the winter, taking the usual precautions by shading and watering, if the weather is dry and hot.

One further piece of advice: do not try, at least at first, to grow lime haters on a limy soil. I know it is done by building up beds of suitable soil, but when one compares the plants in these with those grown in places where the natural soil and water are suitable, it does not seem worth while.

CHAPTER 7

THE EASIER ROCK PLANTS

IT is possible (and do not be ashamed of this) that, for one reason or another, although you wish to grow the dwarf plants usually called rock plants, you do not wish to fuss with the smaller things but want good masses of colour. These you can have and this chapter deals with them. All are of easy cultivation but where one position is preferable to another this will be indicated and if a lime hater, this also. Otherwise they may be expected to grow in any properly prepared rock garden soil.

All the plants mentioned here and throughout are usually obtainable from nurseries but not all from the same one and sometimes, as might be expected, stocks may run out for a season. On principle I do not anywhere mention plants that are very rare or rarely obtainable.

The **Acaenas,** or New Zealand burrs, form widely spreading rooting mats not more than 1 in. high. *A.buchananii* is grown only for its pale pea-green foliage, *A.microphylla* for its bronzy leaves and the showy crimson spines which appear on the flower heads.

Most of the **Achilleas** or yarrows have attractive silvery foliage and white or yellow daisy-like flowers, the branches root as they grow and eventually the plant, unless trimmed, will be 12 ins. across; the flowers are on 6-in. stems. *A.ageratifolia* has narrow silvery leaves and single white flowers; in *A.clavenae* the leaves are silvery and fern-like and the flowers borne in small heads. The hybrid King Edward has almost green foliage and deep creamy-buff flowers. In *A.tomentosa* the foliage is deep green and ferny and the flowers bright yellow; it is one of the parents of King Edward. *A.umbellata*'s leaves are grey rather than silvery and deeply cut, very attractive but the flowers are not as good as those of *A.clavenae*. Plenty of sun for all these, which give pleasure all the year and flower in June.

Most of the **Aethionemas,** which come from the Near East, make quite small bushlets, but there are two bigger ones which make a very considerable show in May–June. *Ae.grandiflorum* and *Ae.theodorum*, which is probably a hybrid, are 12-in. tall bushes of upright stems and as much across, with spikes of small, bright pink wallflower-like flowers. They require the hottest and driest place you can give them.

Most people know the yellow **Alyssum,** *A.saxatile*, from Eastern Europe and it is an excellent plant which gives masses of bright yellow flowers in April–May. Although usually only about 12 ins. tall, it can become 1 ft or more across, but it is wise to cut it back after flowering, for this not only keeps it a better shape but makes it longer lived. Less vigorous but even more showy is the double form *A.saxatile flore pleno*, and smaller is the dwarfer *A.saxatile compactum*. Those who do not like the very bright yellow of the type should grow the pale yellow *A.s.citrinum*, or perhaps the buff Dudley Neville, which I do not like but some do. Plenty of sun for all these.

In the **Androsace** there are several species that are by no means easy, but this is not so in the varieties of *Androsace sarmentosa*, itself a Himalayan plant. By means of strawberry-like runners these make sufficiently large mats to be colourful in May. They have woolly rosettes and heads of round flowers in some shade of pink on 3-in. stems. They are best on a slope in full sun and in wet districts it is wise to cover them with an open-ended cloche or piece of glass held on wires in the winter. *A.s.Galmont*'s var, *primuloides*, *ludlowii* and *watkinsii* are very similar and easy. For other androsaces, see Chapters 8 and 9.

Two **Anemones** are valuable for the lower parts of the rock garden. They are the European *A.narcissiflora*, which has heads of lovely white, pink-backed flowers on 1-ft stems in April–May. *A.magellanica major* from South America is about the same height with single cream or pale yellow flowers; be sure you get the 'major' form as the ordinary is a poor thing.

The **Antennaria**s make mats of grey leaves and from these buttony flowers come on 3–4 in. stems. These flowers are not very attractive except in *A.dioica* Nyewoods, where they are pink. They come from Europe, Asia and North America.

The **Anthemis**, or Chamomiles, are valuable for their mounds of silvery finely cut leaves, above which rise in early summer bright yellow daisies on 6–9-in. stems. *A.biebersteinii* and the similar but smaller and neater *A.rudolphiana*, both from the Caucasus, are suitable for a sunny spot.

The only **Antirrhinum** of value is *A.asarina* from Southern France, which, in a very dry place, preferably a wall, will make a hanging mat with many creamy yellow flowers in the summer. It does need a very dry place and is not a plant for cold gardens.

The genus **Ajuga** includes our common wild Bugle. *Ajuga pyramidalis* is a good plant for a moist position or partial shade; it makes a mat of green leaves and produces in summer many 4-in. leafy spikes, out of which the good blue flowers appear.

To many the word **Arabis** means the rather rampant mat-forming *A.albida*, which is suitable for a wild, stony bank but too spreading even for our purpose. There is, however, a good pink variety *A.a.* Rosabella or *rosea* (I am not sure whether they are the same), which is much neater, only a few inches tall and can be kept in order with trimming. *A.a.coccinea* has deeper pink flowers than the others and a neat habit. The plant listed as *A.aubrietioides* is probably one or other of these pink varieties, as the true plant should be a dense hummock with minute leaves and does not appear to be in cultivation.

Arenaria, the Sandwort, gives us one treasure in *A.montana*, which spreads to make a mat 2 ins. high and 1 ft or more across, but it is a lovely thing when covered with so many pure white flowers in May and June that the foliage is hardly visible. *Arenaria balearica* with minute green leaves and small white flowers spreads freely in a cool moist place, it is excellent for covering damp rocks or peat blocks but in other places may become a nuisance.

No **Artemisia** or Wormwood flowers are of value but they

Oenothera fremontii

Erodium macradenum

Crepis incana

Polygonum affine Donald Lowndes

Saxifraga longifolia

Campanula carpatica

Pulsatilla vulgaris alba

Linum Gemmell's hybrid

take a high place among silver-leaved plants. The rock garden species are European sub-shrubby plants only 1–2 ins. high but spreading reasonably in the sunnier places. *A.baumgartenii* and *lanata* (*pedemontana*) are the best; beware of some others which may spread too vigorously. The leaves are pleasantly aromatic when crushed.

Of **Asperulas** or Woodruffs, *A.hirta* is the only one forming a mat, which is 3 ins. high and valuable for its white flowers turning pink, which appear from July to early autumn; it runs underground, so pieces must be dug out if it gets too big. See also Chapters 8 and 9.

Although I am not a great lover of the European *Aster alpinus* and some of the other alpine asters, they do make good mats from which the daisy-like flowers come on 6-in. stems. It is best to buy selected varieties or hybrids such as Beechwood, mauve-blue, although the white *A.a.albus* is attractive. There are several better ones from China which may reach 12 ins., such as *farreri*, *forrestii* (which is now *A.souliei limitaneus*, but you are unlikely to find it except under its old name), and *likiangensis*.

For dry walls with very little soil and all dry and sunny places, no plants make a more vivid show than the varieties of **Aubrieta** do in March–April. The wild species from Greece and Turkey are now of interest only to the collector. Except where they are in such a dry place that they make very little growth or even go completely brown in summer, they should be cut over with shears or the kitchen scissors after flowering. Lest you become worried, it should be said that these brown mats become green again with the autumn rains. There are semi-double varieties but I do not think the doubling improves them.

Apart from these, there are very many, perhaps too many, varieties of aubrieta from which to choose. I know the following are good but your choice may be as good as mine: Cambria, crimson, Dr Mules, violet blue, Gurgedyke, deep purple, Studland, lavender, Gloriosa, pink, Vindictive, red; or buy a collection from a good nurseryman.

c

The hardy **Calceolarias** are very much neater than the greenhouse fat boys and one or two are good mat-formers for the lower, damper part of the rock beds, in partial shade in hot places. Here they do in full sun. They also have the advantage of flowering in July–August. *Calceolaria acutifolia (polyrrhiza)* makes a low, light green mat with quantities of golden yellow pouched flowers. It spreads freely underground. *C.* John Innes is a hybrid, equally useful but not so freely spreading; the flowers are larger and speckled with brown.

The beautiful **Campanulas,** with their coloured bells or cups, provide several plants for massed colour and are similarly useful for flowering in July–August or even longer. First of all come the varieties of *C.carpathica,* which make ever widening mounds with large floral saucers on 6-in. stems in white or various shades of lavender and mauve. For a start try Blue Moonlight, pale blue, White Star, white, and Isobel, violet blue, and then, if you are as fortunate as I am, self-sown seedlings will appear in all sorts of intermediate shades. Birch hybrid is a good purple-blue 6-in. plant which flowers from May to August.

C.cochlearifolia, which often appears in catalogues as *C.pusilla,* is a real spreader, making foliage mats about 1 in. high and on this myriads of little bells on 3-in. stalks; alba is white, Miranda, very pale blue, and Oakington Blue, darker. The easier sort of rock garden we are talking about here is the only place for this delightful plant for running underground; it can smother choice things. *C.kemulariae* is a more gentle spreader with 6-in. spikes of deep violet hanging bells.

C.poscharskyana I dare hardly mention, as it may become a terrible weed; it is sometimes described as 'robust'. You plant it at your peril, but the Lisduggan variety is much better behaved, and has attractive lavender pink flowers.

C.portenschlagiana, deep violet blue, makes swift or slowly spreading mats which are covered with flower, at least from May to October; it is one of my weeds! See next chapter for the less rampant campanulas.

Ceratostigma plumbaginoides is of value because of its

blue, plumbago-like flowers above bronzy leaves in autumn, when flowers in the rock garden are rather scarce.

No rock garden can do without some **Pinks** or *Dianthus* for their charming July flowers. Among them the varieties of *D.deltoides*, the Maiden Pink, are the best to choose, the colours varying from white to reds and crimson. In sun and a limy soil, they make good tufts, usually about 6 ins. across with flowers on 4-in. stems. Huntsman is a good red, and Wisley variety a good crimson, but the new variety Steriker is the most brilliant of all. They are not long lived but will sow themselves about and probably appear in places where you would never think of putting them.

The Cheddar Pink, which is wild in the Cheddar Gorge of Somerset, suffers now from the terrible name of *D.gratiano-politanus* but thank goodness you may still find it in catalogues as *D.caesius*; the best plant to get is the double form with richly scented double pink flowers. The European *D.arvernensis* is also useful with good pink flowers over a mat of grey foliage. See next chapter for other pinks.

In some gardens the Mountain Avens, *Dryas octopetala*, which, as well as being a British native, grows across Northern Europe and North America, is inclined to make very wide mats of attractive, evergreen, oak-like leaves, but to produce too few of its attractive white, single rose-like flowers. Try it but scrap it if it does not flower freely when it gets 1 ft across, and plant instead the creamy-flowered hybrid *D.sundermannii*, which is more likely to satisfy you. Both flower in May–June. See also next chapter.

There are three strong growing, free-flowering **Gentians** which may be used for colour effect in the easier rock garden, and blue is always acceptable; they do not spread at the root but make an ever widening clump of erect or semi-erect leafy stems ending with large flowers in July–August. These three are *G.gracilipes*, *G.septemfida* and its hybrid *G.x.hascombensis*, and *G.lagodechiana*, which has single flowers at the end of the stem instead of several as the others have. They are all a good intense blue, varying somewhat in shade. *G.gracilipes* comes

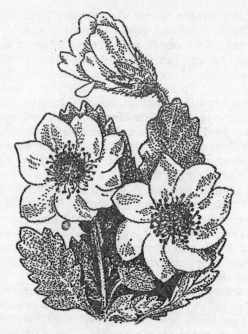

FIG. 4. *Dryas octopetala*

from China, the others from the Near East. All prefer the lower parts of the beds where there is a little more moisture. For the choicer gentians, see chapters 8 and 10.

Geraniums* also provide summer colour and will grow almost anywhere. *G.dalmaticum* with small, shiny, green leaves and soft pink flowers, can become a real ramper and in a wall will work its way through all the crevices, but it is very lovely. There is also a white variety which, as I know it, is a poor thing.

The variety of our wild Bloody Cranesbill, *G.sanguineum*, which grows wild on Walney Island, known as *lancastriense*,

* I mean here the true geranium, which is a hardy plant. The red and pink half-hardy bedding plant of public parks is not properly a geranium, but a pelargonium.

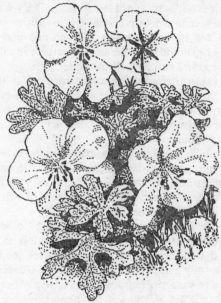

FIG. 5. *Geranium napuligerum (farreri)*

makes a good 2-in. mat and in summer is covered with flesh pink flowers veined in deeper pink; it seldom gets more than 1 ft across. There is also a *G.sanguineum nanum*, dwarfer and less spreading than the original, but you may not like the magenta colour of the flowers.

On the other hand, you will love the Himalayan *G. walli-chianum* Buxton's Blue, with its lovely violet-blue, white-eyed flowers, which has long prostrate branches spreading to about 1½ ft, but which die away to the crown in the winter. All these want plenty of sun. See also next chapter.

Very different from the large herbaceous **Gypsophilas** are *G.repens fratensis* and *G.r.rosea*; both make nice reasonable mounds covered with 6-in. sprays of pink flowers in summer.

Haplopappus coronopifolius is another acceptable plant

because it does not flower until late August. The 1-ft mound of dark green becomes covered with golden daisies on 4–6-in. stems. To look its best it wants full sun and poor soil, i.e. extra sand or grit added to the usual mixture; it will grow in almost pure gravel and look all the better for it.

Helichrysum bellidioides when happy will run about making modest mats 9–12 ins. across and on these in June will come plenty of little white 'everlasting' flowers on 3-in. stems. It is a New Zealander and does not like very cold winters but it does like the sun.

The Horse-Shoe Vetch, *Hippocrepis comosa*, is a native of this country as well as Europe, so there is no point in growing it in the garden, but the variety E. R. Janes has charming, lemon-yellow pea-flowers and comes in usefully with our other spreaders, only a few inches higher.

Some of the **Hypericums,** St John's Worts, make mounds of attractive grey-green foliage 1 ft across and it is no exaggeration to say that in June – August one cannot see the foliage for the large, usually golden flowers, made more attractive by the central boss of stamens. *H.fragile* and *H.polyphyllum* are those usually offered, but if you see the more prostrate *H.rhodopaeum*, with soft, hairy, grey foliage in a list, do not fail to get it.

The perennial **Candytufts (***Iberis***)** have heads of white, four-petalled flowers similar to the annuals, above evergreen foliage. Of *Iberis sempervirens*, sometimes called *I.corraefolia*, Snowflake is the best form, about 9–12 ins. high and 1 ft across, in flower late spring to early summer; the white flowers are of good size. It is essential to prune it after flowering.

I.saxatilis is dwarfer and does not occupy so much space; the flowers, which appear in early summer, become tinged with purple as they grow old.

Several beautiful dwarf **Irises** are at our disposal, most of them coming within the realm of the next chapter. One that belongs here is the American *Iris innominata*, which requires lime-free soil and which makes good mats and is very free with its brown-veined, yellow flowers on stems of 6 ins. or so in

June. There are many hybrids in various colours and all are good. It does not transplant well except as a small plant and if you wish to divide the clump do so immediately the flowers are over, as this is when it starts to make its new roots; do not believe those who say you cannot do this because I and others have.

Leucanthemum hosmarense is a rather new plant with large, white daisies on 6-in. stems above silver-grey, ferny leaves. It will make a good clump and flowers freely in June.

The **Lithospermum** in its various forms offers us some of the most beautiful blue flowers. The most popular, which is shrubby and evergreen and is a mass of small, cup-shaped flowers of some shade of blue in early summer, dislikes lime very much but is indispensable in all other soils. It is *L.diffusum*, which is rather dark in colour, but the varieties Grace Ward and Heavenly Blue are brighter and better. They require full sun, otherwise the 12-in. bushes may become straggly but can always be trimmed if necessary.

L.oleifolium, on the other hand, loves lime and runs about underground when happy. The flowers are a beautiful azure blue on the 3-in. mats of greyish leaves. See also next chapter.

Mazus reptans, although it makes close mats covered with little mauve snap-dragons, should not be placed too near big things as it is only 1 in. tall, but it is a charming little plant.

Mertensia echioides is a true mat-former on which appear sprays of deep violet forget-me-not flowers in summer. Like many Himalayan plants, it does not like too hot a position.

Although they die back to a tuft in the winter the **Evening Primroses** make long, spreading, leafy growths on which in the summer the bright yellow flowers are borne in profusion. In *Oenothera fremontii* the flowers are about 1 in. across, opening about midday, and the leaves are silvery. *O.missouriensis* has green leaves and very large 3–4 in. bright yellow, salver-shaped flowers which open towards the evening and are very effective in the evening light. Both these and *O.oklahomensis*, which is like *O.fremontii* but has red spotted buds, require a dry sunny place.

Some people admire *Omphalodes verna,* which is very like a leafy, dwarf, large-flowered Forget-me-not, but I prefer *O.cappadocica,* which is a lovely blue with large flowers and a good plant for a semi-shady position, where it will run about and seed mildly and flower in late spring and early summer.

A vigorous creeper which likes some moisture but sun is the Shamrock Pea, *Parochetus communis*; if you want to be learned, pronounce the 'ch' like 'k'. The leaves are like the Shamrock and the pea-like flowers are bright blue. I think it wants a sheltered position, as it does not flower until the autumn and even into winter if your garden is not too cold. Put it close to a large rock which will protect its roots.

Several of the American **Penstemons** are excellent little shrub-like plants; they are about 1 ft tall and as much or more across, and evergreen with spikes of little foxglove flowers. They are best trimmed after flowering. *P.barrettae* is bright violet, *scouleri* lilac, and it has a white form, which is not so good (though I think I have a seedling which will be a winner), and Six Hills Hybrid, rosy lilac. Give them the hottest place you have. As well as the trimming, remove most of the seed pods, for one spike of pods will give you all the seed you may want, although you may, of course, give the plant a chance to sow itself if you wish.

In the dwarf **Phloxes** we have some of the easiest, most useful and free-flowering mat-formers for spring display; often there are so many flowers that the leaves cannot be seen. Most of them are varieties or hybrids of the wild *P.subulata* from the eastern U.S.A. They can be white, pink, lavender or crimson and you must make your own choice, but do not omit G. F. Wilson, lavender, Nelsoni, pure white, Betty, pink, and Sampson, rose-pink, which are old and tried varieties, and there are others just as good.

There is a brilliant magenta one, Temiscaming, which I dislike intensely but some love it; they must be colour blind!

P.kelseyi Rosette makes a vigorous mat covered with charming lilac-pink flowers, and although they all like a dry place this appears to require it drier than the others.

There are several other taller phloxes which will spread merrily if happy; they require the moister parts of the rock garden and half-shade in hot places. They are *P.amoena* 6 ins. tall with heads of rose-pink, *P.divaricata* and its variety *laphami*, a lovely shade of lavender and 1 ft tall, and the dwarfer *P.procumbens*, rose-pink or pinky lavender.

Particularly attractive is *P.stolonifera* Blue Ridge with soft blue flowers on 12-in. stems, but it is not the easiest plant to flower in my experience. If you are in a dry place give these a little moss-peat or leaf-mould as well as the half-shade.

The **Polygonums** or knot-weeds give us some terrible weeds, but also three excellent garden plants. The first two make broad mats of fresh green leaves and in summer and early autumn produce tight 2-in. spikes of crimson in *P.affine* Darjeeling Red, while in the newer Donald Lowndes, the spikes open pink then become crimson and later brown. The other, *P.vaccinifolium*, makes mats of small leaves, which will make a perfect fit on a large stone, and in the autumn it covers itself with little pink heather-like flowers. All are Himalayan.

Of the **Potentillas,** with their strawberry-like flowers, the only one I would choose for this chapter is *P.tonguei*, because its flowering stems spread over a foot of ground and the flowers are an unusual apricot with a crimson eye in summer.

There are two **Prunellas** or self-heals which make extensive mats with large hooded and lipped flowers on 6-in. stems. They go under the name of Loveliness, which is lavender, and Pink Loveliness, which is rose-pink. They are probably varieties of *P.webbiana*, of which there is also a white variety. In short, any prunella will suit our purpose as they are strong growers and flower from summer to autumn.

Although they do not spread, the **Pasque flowers** in time grow into such strong clumps that they can hold their own among the other plants I have mentioned. They are all forms of *Pulsatilla vulgaris* (shown in some catalogues by its older name *Anemone pulsatilla*), which in a very diminished form may be found on the sites of some of the old Roman roads in this country. The colours are all shades of lavender, lavender-blue and purple. There are also some excellent whites and reds and pinks, but the reds and pinks I do not find such strong growers and more suitable for the select bed. The buds are most attractive, being covered with silky hairs, their flowers bell- or goblet-shaped, to be followed by lovely fluffy seed heads. It is rare to get so many attractions in one plant. They are, perhaps, happier in lime in the sun than anywhere else.

Some of you may know our wild Bouncing Bet or **Soapwort**, which grows 1–2 ft tall. This is not for the garden, but the European *Saponaria ocymoides* is a good trailing plant covered with flat, pale pink flowers, and one of the easiest of all rock plants. The variety *splendens* is similar, better in colour but not quite so good tempered. Flowers in summer.

Most of the huge family of the **Saxifrages** will be dealt with in the next chapter, but the Mossies are sufficiently vigorous and easy to mention here. They all have lovely mounds of green rosettes in the moister, but not wet, parts of the bed, preferably in half-shade. Some are much more compact than others, such as *decipiens*, white, *moschatus*, white or pink in Stormouth's variety, Pixie, rose-red, and *sanguinea superba*, crimson.

The others are somewhat less compact, but still form nice green mounds and the colours again are white, pink or crimson. There is a pale yellow, very pale, and hardly worth getting, called Flowers of Sulphur. There are so many to choose from that it is difficult to make suggestions but James Bremner, white, Ballawley Guardsman, red, Carnival, rose-pink and Winston Churchill, soft pink, cannot be beaten. Flowers appear in April–May. For other saxifrages, see Chapters 8 and 9.

One **Scabious** with flowers like those of the annuals, but smaller, can be useful for its mats of grey leaves and lilac-pink 'pin cushions' all the summer. It may be bought as *Scabiosa parnassi* or as *Pterocephalus parnassi*, which name is a pity.

Some of the **Scutellarias** or skull-caps are invasive but that does not matter in the bed with which we are dealing. Probably the best is *S.scordifolia*, with the hooded, deep blue flowers on 6–9-in. stems in summer and roots which remind one of false teeth.

The **Sedum,** or Stonecrop, with its fleshy leaves and clusters of bright little flowers, gives us several easy species. In a dry, sunny place in very poor soil, or even on a rock with very little soil, the varieties of *Sedum spathulifolium* will eventually make large masses of rosettes. *S.s.aureum* has yellowish foliage, Capo Blanco, white, *S.s.purpureum* becomes more purple as the season advances, and Wm Pascoe is very like the latter if not identical. All have a dusting of a white meal on the foliage and yellow flowers in June.

Senecio abrotanifolius is common in the Alps of Europe but rare in gardens; it should not be as it makes wide mats of deep green, finely divided foliage from which come lots of orange daisies on 4–6-in. stems.

Few grey-leaved plants produce a better effect than the recently introduced *Tanacetum densum amani* which is usually sold as *Chrysanthemum haradjani*. It will become in time a couple of feet across and the silver leaves are like those of a small and refined fern. The flowers are of no account.

Apart from their scent, the **Thymes** are of great value for making evergreen mats, but they must not be put close to tall plants, as those to which I refer are only 1–2 ins. high and flower in summer. *T.serpyllum albus* has white flowers, Annie Hall is pale pink, *coccineus* crimson, Pink Chintz rose, Bressingham also pink and there is a woolly-leaved variety which goes under the name of *T.s.lanuginosus*.

A good effect is obtained by planting among these a bush or two of the variegated Lemon Thymes *Thymus citriodorus*; of these, *aureus* is bright yellow and Silver Queen, white.

Many of the **Veronicas** are good spreaders and others make large bush-like plants when in flower. Those that are mat-formers offer us a wide choice and it should not be difficult to pick what one likes from the following list.

V.armena rosea, fine leaves, pink flowers, early.

V.cinerea, grey foliage and blue flowers, later.

V.pectinata rosea, woolly foliage and pink flowers in early summer; there is also a scarce blue variety.

In June–August you may have several plants which may be labelled *V.prostrata, rupestris* or *teucrium dubia*; they all mean the same thing. *V.prostrata,* as we will call it, has deep blue 'bird's eye' flowers on short spikes, Mrs Holt and *rosea* are pink, Trehane has golden foliage which looks well among the others and light blue flowers, and the curiously named *bastardii* is china blue. Blue with a red eye which enables you to be sure you have the right thing is *V.saxatilis.*

Bushes up to 9–12 ins. are *V.catarractae,* in blue or white, *incanus,* with silver foliage and spikes of indigo blue flowers in June–July, and *V.prostrata* Shirley Blue and Royal Blue, with masses of bright blue spikes in June.

Never accept as a present or be persuaded to buy *V.filiformis*; if you do you will curse the day you did, for, beautiful as it is, it is a pestilential weed in the garden.

You may put garden **Violas** in the rock garden if you like but I think the large-flowered ones out of place. There are a few which have smaller flowers, are neat in habit and reasonably perennial, if cut back from time to time, to be worth planting, for they have a long flowering season. They are Ardross Gem, blue with yellow centre, Haslemere, pinky lavender (which everyone who visits my garden wants), Hunterscombe Purple, Martin, deep purple, Norah Leigh, lavender blue.

The only species reasonably reliable is *V.cornuta,* with butterflies of lavender or white in the variety *alba* and there is a very dwarf *minor.* The velvety blue *V.gracilis,* is, alas, not a good perennial and I think you will be better with the ones mentioned above, some of which probably have its blood in their make-up.

The last plant for this section is *Waldsteinia ternata* (trifolia) which provides a broad spreading mass of bright green, strawberry-like leaves and flowers with sprays of gold in early summer, only an inch or two high. It is found in Eastern Europe, Siberia and Japan. Its nature is shown by the fact that it is often used as 'ground cover' among shrubs.

I cannot tell you which of all these plants will spread most freely in your garden, so you may have to move them about a bit, or cut back those that are inclined to smother their neighbours, but the loveliest effect is obtained where they just run into each other. You are the artist who must paint the picture. I only give you the paints.

The **Onosmas** are easy, hairy, 6–9 ins. plants for sun and any really dry place. The flowers are in sprays of hanging vases either bright yellow, in *O.tauricum*, or white fading to rose in the grey-leaved *O.albo-roseum*.

CHAPTER 8

CHOICER PLANTS FOR SUN OR HALF-SHADE

ALTHOUGH you may like the masses of colour and foliage effects produced by the easier plants described in the previous chapter you may also wish to have some of the smaller things to enjoy as well. Or, you may be one of those whose sole delight and satisfaction is in these smaller plants; there is no greater pleasure on a quiet Sunday morning or on a summer evening than looking over these little fellows to see how they are progressing; some will be in bud, some in flower and many are attractive even without flower.

They must be treated as important individuals and will appreciate the attention you give them, whether it is watering, top dressing, or removing dead flowers and so on. Most of them are suitable for the pavement if you have one, except the 9–12 in. ones, which look out of place there. As previously, where the plants dislike lime, I will say so, but otherwise any rock garden soil will do.

The first item in this list is a spiny hedgehog (with a rather spiny name) for the hottest place, *Acantholimon gluma-ceum*, the Prickly Thrift. On tight mounds in summer it has pink flowers on 3-in. stems and comes from the Near East. There are others which are seldom available but if you do see them offered buy one. They take some time to make a good mound but, like most slow growers, are long lived.

There are several small, bushy **Aethionemas**, with little wallflower-like blooms and often lovely blue-grey foliage. Being from the Near East, all like it warm and dry. *Ae. pulchel-lum* and *schistosum* are much alike, rose pink in early summer and often again in July and August. The hybrids Warley Rose, Warley Ruber and Mavis Holmes are deeper in colour and, although without the really blue-grey foliage, are first-class plants. If the seed pods are left on the species, self-sown seedlings often appear and are valuable because a bad winter may polish off the parents, when they get old.

The small 3-in. **Alyssums** are much of a muchness, but neat and free flowering in spring and are some shade of yellow, with greyish foliage. Few are offered but *A.montanum* and *wulfenianum* (*ovirense*) appear in lists from time to time.

It is not so long since the **Anacyclus** burst upon the rock gardeners' world, they make tufts of grey-green ferny foliage on which appear large white daisies with red backs, in fact they are better in the bud or half-open rather than fully open. *A.depressus* from Morocco is the one usually offered; give it a hot dry place, and leave a few heads to seed.

The **Androsaces** give us some of the very choicest plants. *A.carnea*, *c.brigantiaca*, *c.halleri* all make green mossy tufts with pink flowers, white in the second one, in spring. They dislike lime.

A.lanuginosa, lilac pink, and its white variety *leichtlinii* have leaves covered with silver fur and the round heads of flower come at the end of 3-in. trailing stems in summer. Best on a really good slope, otherwise cover with a glass in the winter.

A.sempervivoides, being green, does not need this protection; it has small rosettes and heads of pink flowers, a lovely little plant. The last three are Himalayan.

Anemone vernalis is a lovely European pulsatilla, the buds of which are covered with tawny hairs and the flowers are pearly white. It is not difficult to grow, but as it flowers in early spring it must not be in a place where cold winds or drought can shrivel the buds.

Anthyllis montana rubra, the Kidney Vetch or Ladies' Fingers, is a tufted European with hairy, ferny leaves and rosy crimson pea-shaped flowers in round heads and much superior to *A.montana* itself.

There are many dwarf **Columbines** but, like most columbines, they are not usually long lived. I think it best to put them under the less easy plants and therefore mention here only *Aquilegia flabellata nana,* blue, about 6 ins. tall, and its white form *alba.*

Aphyllanthes monspeliensis, for a hot place, gives a different effect as the stems are green and rush-like and blue flowers appear at the ends in summer; if it gets too big you can divide it immediately after flowering.

We have met the **Arenarias** in the previous chapter. A very attractive green cushion is made by *Arenaria purpurascens* covered with lilac-pink stars in spring. Elliott's variety is pinker. A tighter cushion is made by *A.tetraquetra,* the beauty of which is increased by a silver edging to the leaves, the flowers being white. Both these plants come from Spain.

One should always include one or two **Thrifts,** of which the best is *Armeria caespitosa,* making really tight mounds of small leaves on which appear plenty of flowers, pink or white, which in the true plant should sit tight on the tuft, but often the varieties offered have flowers on 1-in. stems and these are almost as good. A plant with 6-in. stems is *A.corsica,* which one grows for its salmon-red flowers.

Silvery leaved plants play an important part in the garden and an **Artemisia** is one of the best. For real silver one cannot beat the ferny leaves of *A.schmidtiana nana* which, like all silver-leaved plants, wants plenty of sun. Liable to be attacked by sparrows.

The **Asperulas** or Woodruffs are real dwarfs. *A.gussonii is* pink, also *A.lilaciflora* and *A.pontica;* both are a particularly fresh green and dotted on the former are deep pink and on the latter rose-pink little tubular flowers. See also Chapters 7 and 9.

Calamintha, which means 'beautiful mint', gives us one or two good plants. *C.alpina* is quite attractive with penstemon-like mauve flowers; better still but taller at 9 ins. is its relation *C.grandiflora,* in which the flowers are rose coloured.

Of the dwarf, non-running **Calceolarias,** the only one available and reliable is the summer flowering *C.biflora,* which has the usual pouched yellow flowers on 4-in. stems. This comes from South America, like most of the calceolarias.

We have seen the more rampant species of **Campanula** in

the last chapter. For our choicer beds there is a tremendous selection; my list of those available has thirty names and this is not including the named garden varieties, but this does not mean that all are easy, so some will appear in a later chapter. Meanwhile, the following are brief notes on some of the leading species and varieties.

There is a group of very neat, tuft-forming plants with large purple bells on 4-in. stems which delight in a hot place but also, alas, are beloved by slugs. They are *C.aucheri, bellidifolia* and *tridentata,* any of which are worth growing for early summer.

Covadonga is a dwarf 'harebell' collected in Spain, with rich purple flowers, and loves plenty of sun, as one would expect.

The varieties of the Italian *C.garganica,* which has radiating stems on which the star-like flowers appear, are all good and love the sun on their greyish leaves, except the blue, white-eyed W. H. Paine, which has green leaves and prefers half-shade.

C.hallii has tubby white bells on a nice green tuft.

C.nitida alba is like a stumpy edition of one of the border campanulas and to me not worth growing.

If you do not object to double flowers, try *C.haylodgensis plena* and R. B. Loder, both pale blue, also *C.warleyensis,* deeper in colour.

C.raddeana has deep violet bells on 9-in. stems and toothed leaves, a good plant from the Caucasus.

C.pulla is a 3-in. gem with satiny, deep violet bells; *C.pulloides* is twice its size, more vigorous and not so good a colour but an attractive plant nevertheless.

C.stansfieldii is a good hybrid of bushy growth and violet bells.

C.tommasiniana and *C.waldsteiniana* make 6-in. tufts of willow-like stems, the former having long violet-blue bells and the latter violet-blue cups. *C.wockii* makes similar bushes with violet bell-flowers.

The plants known as *C.turbinata* are varieties of *C.carpathica* but much neater in growth and therefore suitable to put among the choicer plants; the usual one bears freely, upturned cups of

D

campanula blue and even more beautiful is *C.t.albescens* which is a very, very pale blue. These keep to 4–5 ins.

C.innesii is a hybrid with wide open flowers on gently trailing stems and one must not omit the real purple G. F. Wilson. The advantage of all these campanulas is that they flower in full or late summer and indeed make the main show at this time.

People often fight shy of the **Celmisias,** but most of them are easy to grow in partial shade and, although they come from the peaty moorlands of New Zealand, with me do not object to lime. The one to grow is *C.spectabilis* with silvery leaves or even better *C.spectabilis argentea*, which is an even brighter silver. The large, white, daisy flowers are also attractive.

The American ***Chrysogonum virginianum*** is sometimes offered and, flowering in May, it has its virtues, although the little sun-flowers are not very large; it prefers half-shade.

The pale blue bells of ***Codonopsis ovata*** are more beautiful inside than out, being delightfully and curiously marked with orange and purple; so plant it high so that its stems rest on a rock and you may the more easily look inside.

Be careful of the **Hawkweeds.** *Crepis aurea*, with orange dandelions on 6-in. stems in the autumn, is acceptable, but the gem of the race is the Grecian *C.incana*, which has lots of 1-in. pink dandelions on branching stems about July–August; being Grecian it needs a hot dry place.

The tall **Delphiniums** of the border have some very pretty dwarf relations suitable for the rock garden. *D.grandiflorum* and *D.tatsienense* are rather taller than I like for the small bed, about 12 ins., but their foliage is so light that they may be admitted for their pure blue flowers; of the two, Blue Butterfly is the best colour but the second one is a better perennial, and do not expect them to be long lived. Safer and dwarfer at 9 ins. is the orange, tuberous-rooted *D.nudicaule*, which also has a pale yellow form, daintily borne; it flowers very freely and the colour is vivid but it must have the hottest place possible.

Dwarf **Pinks (*Dianthus*)** are among the choicest plants for summer flowers. I will deal with the species. There are also many garden varieties which may be used without offence if one wishes and these are best dealt with separately.

D.alpinus makes a tuft of green leaves and on these sit 1-in. wide flowers on 1–2-in. stems which are borne with the greatest freedom and it loves lime. The usual colour is some shade of pink with a ring of darker streaks and speckles round the eye. There are paler and darker forms; choose the darkest. There is also a white, interesting rather than particularly beautiful. This gem comes from the Austrian Alps.

D.boydii is presumably a hybrid of the above with similar foliage but the flowers are fringed and it does not set seed.

I cannot write that terrible new name for *D.caesius* (the Cheddar Pink) again, so will say that its double form is neat enough to appear in this section.

D.petraeus (*kitabellii*) is a nice grey mat with scented pink flowers and there is a very fragrant double white form.

D.neglectus can always be spotted because of the buff back to the petals and the bluish eye of the rose-red flowers on 3-in. stems; the leaves are greyish. It is a choice plant from South West Europe and the Tyrol, usually said to dislike lime; maybe people mean chalk, for it grows happily with me and should always be tried as it is one of the choicest species.

Although I cannot find it in any of my very recent catalogues, get *D.nitidus* if it appears, for it is like a smaller *D.neglectus*, but it flowers long after this and goes on for some time with two good rose-pink flowers on each stem. *D.roysii* is an easy variety of *neglectus* which should also be tried.

Of the hybrid pinks, every nurseryman offers different ones and a selection is difficult. There is a warlike quartet of brilliant reds and crimsons – Fusilier, Bombardier, Grenadier and Mars – which are likely to attract you but they are tricky and must be kept going by cuttings. Easier and all sweetly scented are:

Ariel with grey leaves and crimson-cerise flowers.

La Bourbrille and its white form, hybrids of *D.caesius* and as easy to grow, bright pink or white at 3 ins. over grey leaves.

Janet Walker, another good *caesius* hybrid, deep pink.

One should not omit Little Jock which occurred in the garden of a friend, semi-double rose pink and grey foliage.

Nellie Clarke or Mrs Clarke is double crimson and a bit better grower than the War quartet and for a white add White-hills.

Now pinks like lime but they do not like a heavy soil, so if the basic soil of your rock bed is a heavy loam, despite the proper drainage, dig in a little extra sand where you plant these hybrid pinks. See also Chapters 7 and 9.

You probably know the border **Leopard's Bane** with its large yellow daisies in spring, so if you want something similar for the rock garden get *Doronicum cordatum*, which is a minia-ture 8 ins., and the flowers are gold; it wants a nice place at the base of the rock bed but, as it appears to exhaust the soil rather quickly, divide it every two to three years.

There are two good **Dragon's Heads** with spikes of good, blue, penstemon-like flowers, on plants about 9 ins. tall: *Dracocephalum grandiflorum* and *helmsleyanum*, the first coming from Siberia, the second from China. They want a fair amount of room and might have gone into the previous chapter, but they do not like crowding, so give them space in a dry sunny spot. *D.grandiflorum* is the dwarfer of the two.

Dryas octopetala, the Mountain Avens, we met in the last chapter. For this bed, the one to have is *D.o.minor*, very slow growing, like a miniature flattened oak tree bearing small dog-roses.

You will come across the choicest **Edraianthus** in the next chapter, but several will grow in the choice rock bed. They have purple, upright, campanula flowers in clusters at the end of 6-in. stems, spreading from tufts of grassy leaves. They are useful for flowers in June–July and are all very similar; they are *E.dalmaticus*, *graminifolius*, *serbicus* and *tenuifolius*, so get whichever is available.

There are some good willow-herbs, which are **Epilobiums,** and some terrible weeds, including a little bronze carpeter which someone may try to palm off on you, but a new one with the terrible name *E.choraefolium kaikoiensis*, which I assume comes from New Zealand, makes attractive 4-in. tufts of bronze tinted leaves and the flowers are pale or deep pink. Full sun. See also Chapter 10.

I have seen some lovely **Eriogonums** in the drier parts of North America but the best do not like our winters. However, there are two easy plants which are useful for making neat evergreen mats and for flowering in late summer, the flowers being in close heads at the top of 6–9 in. stems. *E.umbellatum* is pale yellow and *E.subalpinum*, white fading to pink. Give them plenty of sun.

For the sunny rock garden few plants are of greater value for summer flowers and a long summer at that, than the **Erodiums** or Heron's Bills, so called because of the way the seed pods

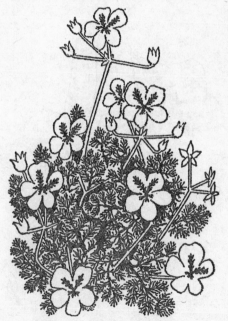

FIG. 6. *Erodium guttatum*

stick out like a beak. The following make tufts of ferny leaves which are beautiful in themselves: *E.amanum*, white flowers faintly lined pink, *E.chrysanthum*, pale yellow, and *E.macradenum* white, pink striped with a purple peacock-eye on the two upper petals. Hot and dry for these.

The **Erysimums** are like miniature wallflowers and the lilac *E.linifolium* is no longer lived than the bedding wallflowers although a really dry place will help it, as will be understood when you hear it comes from Spain. On the other hand *E.rupestre* (*pulchellum*), also I believe appearing as Sprite, is much longer lived; in spring the 2-in. mats are covered with primrose wallflowers.

We saw some of the easier **Gentians** in the previous chapter. For our choicer bed there are two of the most beautiful of

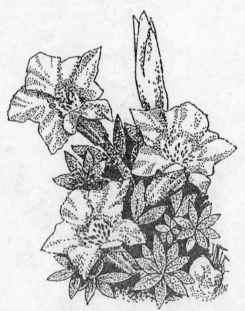

Fig. 7. *Gentiana acaulis*

the genus. Perhaps the most celebrated is the gentianella, *Gentiana acaulis*, with large, superb trumpets of a vivid dark blue. This is one of those plants which (like the Madonna lily) grows easily enough in many gardens but in others refuses to flower or flowers but feebly. It likes being planted *firmly* in stony, limy loam and to have plenty of water in the spring to prevent the buds going blind.

If the ordinary form fails with you, try *G.a.coelestina*, *undulatifolia* or *dinarica*, all just as beautiful and one or the other is reasonably sure to like your garden.

G.verna, the star gentian, although not usually long lived, must be grown for its lovely star-like flowers of intense blue, best in the variety *angulosa*, even if occasional replacement is necessary. This needs, in contrast to the gentianella, a moist, sandy, peaty soil in sun and therefore is best suited at the bottom of the bed. For other gentians, see Chapters 7 and 10.

Several **Geraniums** deserve a place in this section as they are low-growing, tufted and have large flowers. *G.argenteum*, a treasure of the Dolomites, has lovely silvery leaves and the flowers are soft pink, veined.

G.cinereum is grey, not silver, and the pinkish flowers are also veined with a darker shade. This is a Pyrenean plant. It varies considerably and its brightest form goes under the name of *G.subcaulescens* or *subcaulescens splendens*, having very showy carmine flowers with a dark eye, whereas the ordinary variety is lighter in the centre.

There is a new and good geranium called Ballerina, which is related to the above with flowers of a delightful shade of pink.

You all know the garden **Geums** but probably not the alpine *G.montanum*, a neat tufted plant with good bright yellow 1–1¼ in. 'single roses' in early summer followed by charming fluffy seed-heads. It has no fads.

The **Globularias,** as you will guess, have round heads of flower usually some shade of what may be called 'steely blue' or sometimes 'powder blue'. There are some pink or white varieties, but none of those I have seen are worth growing. The following are the good ones.

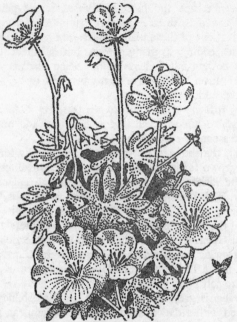

Fig. 8. *Geranium subcaulescens*

G.bellidifolia is a 1-in. evergreen tuft and the globes sit on it. *G.cordifolia* is really a little shrub which will crawl over any rock and make it attractive with its small evergreen leaves even without the flowers on 3-in. stems. *G.nudicaule* and *trichosantha* are taller, 6 ins. or so, and have larger heads. All are South European except the last, which comes from Asia Minor and flowers in summer.

The little **Gypsophilas** are charming. *G.cerastioides* is only 1 in. tall and the tufts bright with white purple-veined flowers. *G.dubia* is prostrate with bronzy leaves and small pink flowers. Very like *G.repens fratensis* (see Chapter 7), the cumbrously named *G.franzii nana compacta* is very neat with good pink flowers. All these flower in summer.

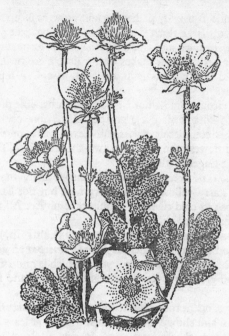

FIG. 9. *Geum montanum*

Heliosperma alpestris, which is also Silene, has pure white flowers like a little pink but the leaves are glossy. This is one of the few flowers in which the double form is more attractive than the single, and really very beautiful.

The **Hutchinsias** are useful for their neat cushions of evergreen, finely cut leaves. The white flowers of *H.alpina* are small but borne in profusion in late spring and *H.auerswaldii* is similar. They prefer the moister places at the base of the rock garden or the partial shade of a rock.

We have seen several of the dwarf, golden **Hypericums,** or St John's Worts, in the last chapter and here we have several more. *Hypericum olympicum* can come in here, for instead of large mounds, it usually makes upright growths of up to 12 ins. crowned with large flowers of gold in the type, pale yellow in the variety *citrinum*, and there is also a *minor* form suitable for the smaller bed. *H.coris* makes pretty little 6-in. bushes like a heather and the flowers again are gold, as are all the normal hypericums.

H.repens from Asia Minor is another heather-like plant, and, in spite of its name, is not a creeper! *H.reptans*, on the other hand, makes completely flat, small-leaved mats, on which sit the golden flowers the size of a two-shilling piece, the outer parts being tinged with red.

Hypericum trichocaulon, another mat-former, has bronze buds and starry yellow flowers, very neat but not hardy with me, so those in cold districts should take notice. All are good for summer bloom.

As well as the big **Candytufts** already dealt with, there are several good miniatures such as *Iberis sempervirens* Little Gem, 6 ins., and one called *I.pygmaea*, which is quite flat on the ground and grows but slowly. All are evergreen and flower in spring.

The large, open, rose-pink trumpets of the **Incarvilleas** are so beautiful and showy that one must include at least *I.grandiflora*, in which the flowers open at ground level and then elevate themselves on 6-in. stems; the plant is 12 ins. across, so give it fair space.

The varieties of *I.mairei* recently introduced are dwarfer but scarce and not yet well tested. They flower in summer and die away entirely to a carrot in the winter.

Many of the most beautiful small **Irises** carry on the theme of this chapter. *Iris cristata* from North America and its smaller brother *I.lacustris* both like the shadier side of the rock garden or the moister part towards the bottom. If some extra moss-peat is forked in the latter will grow quite satisfactorily on lime soil. I am almost but not quite sure about the former. The flowers are blue, lilac and gold in the spring.

In *Iris pumila*, if true to name, the relatively large flowers in white, blue, purple or yellow are almost stemless and the whole plant only 3–4 ins. tall and excellent in May for the driest place you have, particularly on lime. *I.mellita* is similar in size, smoky purple or yellow. More often the plants of *Iris pumila* offered by nurseries are varieties of *I.chamaeiris*, the flowers of which are on 6-in. stems, the range of colour being the same.

It is often stated that these two require division every two years because they exhaust the soil. With the feeding advocated in Chapter 6, I do not find this necessary. Nature does not divide them but, of course, if they get crowded, do so, and do it soon after the flowers have faded, as they then begin to make new roots; in any event not later than the end of June.

Another dwarf sometimes offered is the Himalayan *Iris kumaonensis*, 6 ins., which is worth growing because the flowers are mottled lilac, unlike any other. It likes the moister parts low down.

Iris ruthenica is also dwarf at flowering time in May, and the effect of the mixture of colours is reddish violet and white and, unusual for an iris, the flowers are fragrant; this also should be planted on the lower levels. In the wild this plant is found from Eastern Europe and on to China.

For a similar position one may try *I.graminea*, which smells of ripe plums, but the bright violet flowers are much hidden by the foliage.

Iris setosa also covers a wide region from Eastern Siberia to North America. There is a dwarf variety with purple flowers which is worth seeking.

People may have lost their lives trying to clutch the odd **Edelweiss** flower, seeing it hang down from a precipice, but if they had looked round they would have found they could walk on yards of it. Moreover, *Leontopodium alpinum* is by no means the best of the Flannel Flowers.

I find that much superior are the 6-in. *L.stracheyi* and *L.sibericum*, which is an extremely good white, the best I have so far. *L.soulieiei* is only about 4 ins. and the flowers are smaller. *L.haplophylloides* is not much to look at but the crushed leaves give off the scent of lemon. Plenty of sun for these.

The **Lewisia**, looking rather like a glorified daisy, is a rock genus of outstanding beauty. The fleshy leaved plants, from North America, make a great show in pink, red, peach, coral and apricot, often striped with red; that is to say, the hybrids do. Few of the original true species are now available, and you cannot do better than start with a few of these hybrids.

What lewisias hate whole-heartedly is winter wet, so plant them on a raking slope, preferably in crevices between stones with 2–3 ins. small gravel under their rosettes. It has been said that they dislike lime; that is not true of limy loams, for they grow well in the Cotswolds but possibly they might fail in real chalk. It is also suggested that they are short-lived, yet in Bodnant Gardens there are huge clumps 1 ft across planted in holes in the terrace walls, and these must be veterans!

One associates **Flaxes (*Linum*)** with blue but, apart from

FIG. 10. *Linum toxicum*

the prostrate blue *L.alpinum*, which I find short-lived, the best for the rock garden are yellow. The 9-in. bushlet of *Linum arboreum* is lovely when covered with clear yellow flowers in summer but either I am unlucky or it is not hardy with me; however, *L.toxicum* from the Lebanon, which is very similar, seems unaffected by our Cotswold weather; so if you fail with the first, try the second.

But *L.arboreum* has left a most lovely child, known as L. Gemmel's hybrid, 4 ins. high, which covers itself with clear butter yellow, real butter, flowers in May; nobody has yet been able to tell me in what home this child was born.*

The 12-in. *L.campanulatum* and *L.flavum* are not quite so distinguished but are nevertheless valuable for giving heads of deep yellow flowers all the summer, set off by the grey-green leaves. Plenty of sun for all Linums.

The **Lithospermums** we have already met in the last chapter. Two other good ones will be found under moltkia but most catalogues still stick to the old and more familiar name. *L.graminifolium*, which is *Moltkia suffruticosa* (I apologise but am trying to help you find them), makes tufts of long narrow grass-like leaves and sprays of blue flowers. *L.intermedium*, or *M.intermedia*, is taller and deep blue. They love lime and full sun, both flower in summer.

Lychnis alpina is a Scottish native, neat but rather un-assuming with small heads of dull crimson. I grow it, though it never excites me, but it seeds freely and I am always hop-ing that one day an astonishing pure pink child will appear. Tufts of narrow green leaves and little heads of flower at about 3 ins.

Mertensia pterocarpa (*rivularis japonica*) is the best of the mertensias available. The heart-shaped leaves are a lovely blue-grey above which are sprays of little sky-blue bells; in half-shade it is one of my successes and pops children about here and there.

The **Micromerias** make no great show but are plants which

* I now know, it occurred as a spontaneous hybrid in the display border of R. K. Gemmell and Co., Blairside, Kilwinning, Ayrshire.

one likes to pinch when passing because of the scented foliage. *Micromeria corsica* is grey leaved and unscented, *M.piperella* green and *M.varia* bronzy, but what I was given as this is, I believe, *M.graeca* and a good plant. They appear to be confused in catalogues. All flower in late summer, pinky-lilac. They are plants for sun and drought.

Moltkia petraea is a true moltkia and shrub-like; it is a rare plant and I am very doubtful of its hardiness away from the south and west, so we will say no more about it.

There are many interesting **Forget-me-nots** apart from the ones you know so well and most of these come, or rather we should like them to come, from New Zealand. At present we have only one available, *Myosotis explanata*, which is a gentle mat-former and the flowers are pure white, not blue, in early summer. Half-shade.

The naming of the **Evening Primroses (*Oenothera*)** is in many instances a bit of a mix-up, so I must use those met with in the catalogues. As indicated by the common name, most of them open in the cool of the evening, when they shine in the twilight and have faded by the midday following.

O.acaulis has large white flowers on 6-in. stems fading to pink, but in the variety *aurea* they are yellow.

O.flava makes a tuft of green dandelion-like leaves and it sends up a long succession of large yellow flowers from July onwards. The brown, horny seed pods remain on the plants for a long time, and self-sown seedlings occur freely, with me in a gravel path.

O.pumila (*perennis*) Sundrops, has small, deep yellow blooms in sprays, day flowering, high summer.

O.riparia, a form of *O.tetragona* of which there are many varieties dwarf and tall, makes a mass of slender growths up to 12 ins. of narrow leaves and 1-in. bright yellow blossoms. Contrary to most evening primroses, it prefers a cooler position or half-shade. See also the previous chapter.

The good **Oxalis** are very good plants, and the bad, very bad weeds. They really come under tuberous rooted plants but as they usually appear in plant catalogues I am putting them in here. The good ones come from South America, mainly at the cold end.

O.adenophylla from Chile has a curious, net-covered root, the tufted leaves look as if crimped and the flowers, which appear in May, are upright lilac-pink bells. Full sun for this.

Very similar in foliage and flower shape is *O.enneaphylla* but the large flower is glistening white, though there are pale, deep pink and rose-red varieties. These come from Patagonia and the Falkland Islands and like half-shade better than full sun and flower in May.

O.depressa, which has been *inops* and *convexula*, poor thing, is a Basutoland plant, its leaves clover-like and the flowers rose pink; it can, when happy, become a nuisance by running too freely underground.

The Alpine poppy, **Papaver alpinum,** is a charming ferny-leaved plant with small poppies, white, pink, yellow or orange on 3-in. stems; it does not live long with us but leaves many children, who can be removed if in the way. The best way to grow this is to scatter a packet of seed over the sunny parts and await the flowers, which will go on all the summer.

Patrinia triloba is not a common plant but it is an extremely useful one because it flowers from July to September; it makes tufts of bronzy green, maple-like leaves and the heads of fragrant golden-yellow flowers are on 6-in. stems. It is one of the few members of the valerian family which is any use to us. It requires half-shade.

For the dry sunny garden the **Penstemons** are invaluable. Some are apt to be short-lived, or it may be that we have not yet solved their wants, but the ones that follow should offer no difficulty if, apart from sun, they are planted high so as to get the most perfect drainage. The flowers are miniatures of the big garden ones and they all come from the west of North America.

From a mat of small leaves the blue flowers of *P.albertinus* come on 6-in. stems. The true *P.davidsonii* runs about slowly underground and has large ruby-red flowers almost sitting on the foliage. *P.hallii* makes a low mat like the first mentioned and the flowers on 6-in. stems are blue or violet. *P.menziesii* and *m.microphyllus* make an evergreen mat hugging the ground and the large, lavender blue flowers sit on this; the second has much smaller leaves.

P.newberryi humilior is a little 6-in. shrubby plant which I have seen in California lining the crevices of huge granite boulders with masses of rosy-crimson flowers. The best place to put it is behind a stone, so that it can spread over it. This is often sent out wrongly as *P.roezlii*, which has blue or mauve flowers. There are two good hybrids of this, named Weald Beacon and Grasmere Beauty, with more blue in the flowers.

P.rupicola is a prostrate plant with ruby-red flowers and often does duty for the true *P.davidsonii*.

P.pinifolius has vivid scarlet flowers on little heather-like bushes; the introducer, Professor Worth of New York, never expected that it would be an easy garden plant and yet it is, so you never know.

Sometimes a *P.coloradense* is offered; I find this particularly attractive, a little spreading bush with narrow leaves and 6-in. erect spikes of open-mouthed foxgloves, blue with a white throat on opening, fading to mauve.

My advice is get any dwarf penstemon you see offered except *P.confertus* (*procerus*) which is a poor yellowish-white cluster head. All flower in May–June.

Although the **Phloxes** dealt with in the previous chapter are beautiful, the more dainty members now to be mentioned are, if it is possible, even more so. Contrary to all the others, *P.adsurgens* must have partial shade or a cool place and an extra handful of moss-peat or leaf-mould when planting, as it grows at the edge of pine-woods which are always deep in leaf-mould; although it definitely prefers an acid soil it will grow on lime if the above advice is taken. It is a trailer with real salmon-pink flowers and a white eye.

Phlox bifida is a spiny-leaved bush 6–8 ins. tall, the flowers being white and deeply cut, hence 'bifida'; really hot for this.

P.caespitosa and J. A. Hibberson and *diffusa* are tight little 1–2-in. mats excellent in the pavement; the flowers of the former pale lilac, the latter very pale blue as also is *P.hoodii*, the smallest of the lot.

P.brittonii rosea is equally dwarf but will make a mat up to 10 ins. across and the flowers which come later, in June–July (the others in May), are a lovely pink.

Phlox douglasii is the easiest dwarf one for the choice bed, so covered with flowers in May that you cannot see the leaves; whether the plants we can get are the true wild plant is doubtful but that does not matter, you will like them anyway. Get Beauty of Ronsdorf, deep mauve, Boothman's variety, mauve with a deep eye, Eva, pink with a crimson eye, May Snow (you will guess the colour), *rosea*, pink, and Violet Queen and any others you see advertised. All these precious phloxes must have it hot and dry.

The **Platycodons** or balloon flowers, so called from the shape of the buds which open into large campanulas, are, all except one, plants for the herbaceous border and this one, which came from Mt Apoy in Japan, is only about 6 ins. high. It has several names of which *P.apoyensis* is probably the most correct. Besides being a good plant it is useful for flowering in August.

Again Jacob's Ladders are mostly for the border but one may come here and it is *Polemonium reptans*, with 9-in. deep-blue flowers. There are some lovely but more difficult Americans which will appear in the next chapter.

Our native Milk Wort's bright blue, pink or white flowers can be seen on the chalk downs; it is *Polygala calcarea*, for limy gardens. Get a good plant of the blue and let it sow itself where it will, it is charming and no nuisance.

The one **Polygonum** that keeps itself to itself is the spring flowering *P.tenuicaule*, a clump former on which the heart-shaped leaves appear after the little spikes of white flowers. Half-shade for this. The more rampant 'Knot-weeds' are in the previous chapter.

There is a goodly number of **Potentillas**, yet many seem just 'to miss the bus' and I do not wish you to clutter the garden with doubtful subjects, but I think you will like

E

P.aurea plena, which makes little mats of bright-green strawberry leaves and then double yellow 'roses' in spring.

P.cuneata (*ambigua*) and *P.eriocarpa* run about slowly and, on and off in summer, produce single rose-like golden flowers. They are Himalayan.

P.nevadensis is a little Spaniard, neat and yellow.

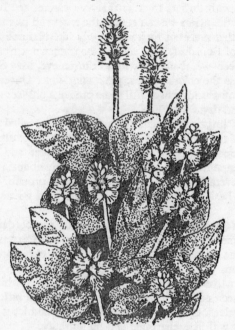

FIG. 11. *Polygonum tenuicaule*

P.nitida is the gem of the race with silver-grey mats studded with soft, deep pink little 'dog roses'. The problem is to get it to flower freely, some forms being better than others in this respect. Give it full sun and plant so that it rests on a rock, the warmth of which helps to ripen the growth, and may help it to flower.

P.rupestris pygmaea gives another change of colour in grey foliage and white flowers, about 6 ins. in all.

P.verna nana is an easy miniature yellow one for early summer, when it is covered with blossom, the little plant remaining trim and green.

There are several others which it is as well to see before buying. Remember also *P.tonguei* in the previous chapter.

We come now to one of the most beautiful of flower families – the **Primula.** There is a host of rock, as opposed to bog or damp soil, primulas, but the many European species and natural hybrids are not easy to bring to flower in the open. The following are however usually reliable.

The wild *P.auricula* of the European Alps is far too seldom seen; the flowers are yellow, sweet scented and the leaves mealy, more or less, but be sure it is one of the wild forms, not the garden hybrids referred to later.

The next one which offers no difficulty about flowers is *P.marginata* from the Maritime Alps. The toothed leaves are mealy, particularly at the edge, and the flowers are of good size and in all shades of lavender, lilac and purple. There are numerous named varieties and they are all good, particularly Linda Pope. It is natural for them to get leggy, so preferably plant between two rocks so that they can hang down. They can, however, be grown on the flat but, if so, as the stems get long, pack them round with small stones, among which they will eventually make nice clumps.

Although I do not recommend the garden auriculas for the rock garden, as they look rather out of place, the hybrids of *P.auricula* crossed with several other wild species are excellent and suitable plants. Try Faldonside, deep crimson, Mrs J. H. Wilson, violet, and The General, terracotta, all old stagers, and there are several newer ones worth trying, and if you see it in a catalogue or otherwise do not miss the exquisite white one, *P.pubescens alba.* In hot gardens these hybrids need half-shade, as also does one of the wild parents, *P.rubra* which is good if in a nice colour form; it varies a lot. See also Chapter 10.

I have referred to *Pulsatilla vernalis* under anemone, very

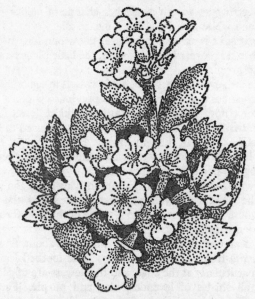

FIG. 12. *Primula pubescens alba*

wrong I know, so now I will refer to the largest of these plants as **Pulsatilla alpina** and *P.a.sulfurea*, which sometimes grow in the European Alpine meadows as buttercups do here. They grow up to 12 ins. tall and the flowers are large, white with a blue reverse in the former, yellow in the latter.

They do not transplant well and should always be put in as young seedlings, which means you will have to wait 3–4 years for them to flower, but then they will live for ever or a very long time, and are such lovely plants that they are worth waiting for. In nature the former grows only on limestone, the latter usually but not always on acid soils, but in the garden they do not appear to mind, but put them low down, as they require 1 ft of room.

The **Ranunculus** is the Buttercup family and the rock gardener has some pretty things to choose from it. *Ranunculus*

FIG. 13. *Ranunculus amplexicaulis*

amplexicaulis, at 6 ins., with 1–1¼ in. wide pure white flowers, is one of the glories of the north and south Pyrenean meadows; it is slender but put it low down in sun or half-shade as it likes a little moisture. When happy it will seed about freely and extra good forms, such as semi-double, may appear and be selected and sometimes a seedling will have a touch of pink. Flowers in May.

There is a charming hybrid, *R.x.arendsii*, between this and the golden *R.gramineus*, with cream flowers, but as far as I am concerned it does not grow happily.

R.calandrinioides is a remarkable plant for it is bone hardy and yet it comes from the Atlas Mountains of Morocco. It usually dies away in the summer and the attractive wavy grey-green leaves reappear with the autumn rains and the white, pink-tinged flowers in January–March. The petals are rather thin and the flowers not always of perfect shape, but it varies greatly and there are some good forms about, so if possible see the plant before you buy it. I think it a plant with great possibilities for improvement by some energetic amateur.

R.gramineus is very like a refined buttercup and one does not need it unless a large-flowered variety comes forward.

R.montanus (*geraniifolius*) is a tufted little plant, in effect a very dwarf Buttercup of about 4 ins. There is a variety called Molten Gold but I am not sure that it is so much better than a reasonably good form of the original.

Raoulia australis is really like a splash of molten silver and is grown for this effect of the minute leaves. It does not like me, whether because of cold or lime, but perhaps it is my fault and it has not been planted high enough in the sun and given a chance to spread over a rock. I have still to try it for the third time in my present garden. There are several other raoulias all from New Zealand but none to beat this.

Down at the bottom of the rock garden slopes put **Roscoea humeana.** It will not appear until May or even June and then up shoots some broad green leaves and from the top of the 10–12-in. stem large, lipped, rich purple flowers keep popping up, as many as ten from the one stem.

R.cautleoides is usually nearer 12 ins. and the flowers, similar in shape, are a charming pale yellow.

R.alpina, sometimes offered, is, as far as I have seen it, what a friend of mine calls a 'little misery'.

The Soap Wort, or **Saponaria,** give us several excellent plants which must be high up with plenty of sun or on a steep slope or in a crevice. *Saponaria* Bressingham hybrid is like a compact bright coloured *S.ocymoides* (see previous chapter) in May–June. *S.ocymoides rubra compacta* is a wonderful coloured miniature of *S.ocymoides* but it is a tricky beast and must be dry and is so scarce that it is worth putting a glass over it in the winter, when its constitution is under the greatest strain; perhaps it should come in the next chapter.

S.x.olivana, however, is good tempered and in May–June the green tuft surrounds itself with a ring of lilac-pink blossoms and, when these have faded, what looks like a nest full of little rusty-red and green eggs is left.

Autumn plants are always valuable in the rock garden and when the leaves are aromatic, doubly so, such as **Satureia subspicata**, with violet flowers in September; this is one of the Savorys, of which the Summer Savory is used for seasoning pork pies and various sauces. *S.repanda*, white, is equally useful for this month.

One hardly knows where to begin with the vast family of the choicer **Saxifrages.** My list of what are called the 'silvers' contains fifty names and I think I will confine myself to these here. The so-called Kabschias and Englerias can be grown in the rock garden, but are more easily managed in a scree or pavement and are accordingly placed in Chapter 9.

The silvers are so called because the leaves of the rosettes, which is the way they are arranged, are silver-grey with lime and silver at the edges which have little pits plugged with lime. The rosette which has flowered always dies but numerous daughter rosettes develop round this.

Saxifraga aizoon is the most widely distributed in Nature and consequently very variable, particularly in the size of the rosettes; and further confusion is caused by the fact that all these silvers hybridize very readily in the garden; they do not get the same chance in the wild. My list of *S.aizoon* contains sixteen varieties as available but a few select ones will do for the ordinary garden. The flowers, in sprays from 2–6 ins. or so long, vary from dirty white, good whites, heavily spotted, pink and yellow.

The smallest, with tiny rosettes, is *S.a.baldensis* and the largest *S.a.Rex*. *S.a.balcana* is so heavily spotted with red that it appears almost that colour. *S.a.lutea* is an attractive pale yellow with 6-in. sprays and *S.a.rosea* pink of about the same height.

All the forms of *S.cochlearis* are good, making small humps of rosettes up to 1 in. across.

S.cotyledon is one of the larger kinds, with broad-leaved rosettes up to 4–5 ins. diameter and 12-in. sprays of pure white flowers, or variously spotted.

S.c.pyramidalis has pure white flowers, whereas *S.c.*'Southside Seedling' is so heavily spotted as to appear red.

According to my experience the northern forms which go under the names of *icelandica* or *norwegica* dislike lime, anyway they died on me; all the others love it.

The varieties of *S.lingulata, albida (albertii)* and *lantoscana* from the Maritime Alps are better than the parent species, as the flowers are a very pure white.

S.longifolia can be seen making large rosettes in the crevices of cliffs in the Pyrenees with sprays of white flowers up to 2 ft in length, but unfortunately it dies after flowering and leaves no youngsters; therefore it is best to grow what are probably hybrids. Walpole's variety is good but Tumbling Waters and Symons Jeunii are staggering in their 2-ft plumes of white flowers.

S.kolenatiana, with pointed leaves, is of interest because the flowers are pink on 12–16-in. sprays; *S.sendtneri* is the best form of it and the leaves of the dying rosette go a rich crimson.

Always worth having are several of the smaller hybrids with 6-in. sprays. I like Dr Ramsay, white dotted pink and reddish leaves in autumn, Francis Cade, pure white, and the pink Kathleen Pinsent, the silver rosettes of which are only 1–1½ ins. across. There are many others which you may care to have when you wish to increase your collection.

One little **Scabious** is suitable for our choice bed; it is *Scabiosa graminifolia*, which makes compact tufts of narrow, silvery leaves and during the summer produces a succession of pink pincushions on about 6-in. stems. In spite of its formidable name, which must not frighten you off, I am very fond of the Eastern Europe *Schivereckia podolica* with its 6–8-in. tufts of grey-green rosettes, covered with little white wallflowers on 2–3-in. stems in spring.

At one time I was inclined to turn up my nose at **Sedums**, or Stonecrops; a bit of horticultural snobbishness, because they

are so easily grown! Now I find their leaves and often their
flowers very attractive and for dry places on the tops of rock or
dry walls, in the sun, they are most valuable, but you must
make a careful choice.

Sedum cauticola makes bluish pink-edged leaves on stems
which end in carmine heads of flower in autumn. *S.lidakense*
and *S.pluricaule* are similar and good. They are, I believe, all
Japanese.

S.douglasii is a mound of fleshy green topped with heads of
yellow, with perhaps a trifle too much green in the colour.

S.oregonum has rosettes of fat little leaves which colour well
in the autumn or earlier depending on the season.

S.spurium Schorbusser Blut is grown for its bright red
flowers in late summer; it is more of a mat former than the
others, which make tufts. See the previous chapter for other
Stonecrops.

The House Leeks or **Sempervivums** I must admit are not
among my favourite plants but here again they are useful for
the tops of rocks and dry walls. The most attractive are the
varieties of *S.arachnoideum* because the rosettes are covered
with cobweb-like hairs; to these I would add *S.ciliosum*, with in-
curved hairy leaves, Malby's hybrid, with large mahogany-red
rosettes and the also red *S.ornatum* (schlehanii), and possibly
the fat boy of our native house-leek called *S.calcareum robus-
tum*. If you wish for more, some catalogues are full of them.

I have found ***Silene keiskii minor*** most attractive, forming
6-in. mounds of narrow bronzy leaves and pink flowers in late
summer, and although it vanishes in the winter it reappears in
spring.

There are several **Sisyrinchiums**, which are like little iris
tufts with blue or yellow flowers in summer. They are pretty
little plants and will usually seed about and are useful for an
odd corner. *S.bermudianum* is violet-blue, and *S.brachypus*
yellow, but the gems are *S.grandiflorum* (*douglasii*), which has
tufts of rush-like leaves and hanging bells of reddish purple or
white in early spring, and *S.odoratissimum* with similar leaves,
trumpet flowers, white or cream, often pencilled with purple

and delightfully scented in June. It is about 9 ins. tall whereas *S.filifolium*, also from South America (Falkland Islands), is only 6 ins. and prefers a moister soil with a little peat, so put it lower down than the former, which is not so particular.

There are two miniature **Golden Rods** useful for late flowers. *Solidago brachystachys* is about 6 ins. and Golden Thumb about 9 ins. I have to emphasize the value of plants which flower late in the season, as by then the majority of rock plants are setting seed before going to rest for the winter.

Stachys lavandulifolia is another flower for late summer, a grey mat with fluffy, purplish, lipped flowers in small spikes. It wants a hot dry place and so far I have failed with it here, and wonder whether it is reliably hardy. Try it in full sun and a dry place.

Trachelium rumelianum, from Greece, belongs to the campanula family, although you would not think so. Apart from the beauty of its fuzzy heads of lilac-blue these have the virtue of appearing in August.

Tunica saxifraga is not a very distinguished plant, having small pink flowers very like a poor gypsophila; very much better is the double form Rosette which gives a charming display of pretty pink blossoms on slender stems in summer.

In the **Veronicas**, as seen in the previous chapter, we have a most valuable family of plants, but there are a few neater ones which may come in here. Those inclined to be sub-shrubby are sometimes called hebes, but the true shrubby hebes will appear in the chapter on Dwarf Shrubs.

V.bidwillii is a 3-in. mat of extremely small leaves and white flowers on very slender stems, *V.catarractae* is more robust with white or blue flowers.

There is a charming little, pink-flowered, Japanese plant going under the name of *V.bandaiana* which flowers in May, but it may also be blue. This blue form came to me as *V.schmidtiana* but I believe they are the same species so buy under either name; masses of 3-in. spikes in May.

V.selleri is another very dwarf plant with 3-in. spikes of deep blue in July–August, whereas *V.saturioides* is in flower in

April; this makes a completely prostrate mat with 1-in. spikes of bright blue flowers, good for being the first veronica to flower, but it does not last very long.

The **Zauschnerias** are gay and charming where they are hardy but I have my doubts about this, as they have failed in my cold garden; this is not surprising, as they come from the warmer states of the USA. They give a wonderful finish in September to the rock garden season. If your garden is reasonably warm and dry, try them in the hottest, driest place you have and you will be delighted with their scarlet tubular flowers. *Z.californica* is scarlet with greyish hairy leaves, *Z.cana* (*microphylla*) has its leaves almost silver and similar flowers.

If you succeed with a goodly number of the plants I have here described you will be well on the way to be ready to try those more difficult ones requiring the conditions of the scree to which we come next. Hasten slowly is an old but excellent maxim for gardeners.

CHAPTER 9

PLANTS FOR SCREE AND ASH BEDS

A FAMOUS and skilful cultivator of rock plants recently wrote that if he had to start a rock garden again he would furnish it almost exclusively with screes or peat beds. Not having tried all the rock plants I have grown at one time or other in scree beds, I would not go as far as this, as some probably like the more meaty soil of the rock garden better and certainly many, very many in my experience, dislike peat; also a nicely built rock bed is attractive to look at when the plants are in and it cannot be said that a scree is a thing of beauty.

There is, however, something to be said for the idea of a garden of screes in places where rock is difficult to come by, material for screes usually being readily available, and I would hazard a guess that most of the plants talked of in the previous chapter would grow, excepting where I have suggested 'moist'.

So if you have no rock make a series of scree beds, some with more soil than advised in Chapter 5 and some with less, but you will have to attend to the watering more regularly, except for the bed for plants where I have said 'hot and sunny'.

However, now I am going to talk about the plants that must have a scree if they are to grow at all or are better in it; better in the sense that they grow better, live longer or keep a neater, compact habit which they lose in the richer soil of the rock garden. They, on the whole, are not plants to try until you have had some experience, although plants are so unpredictable that you, if a beginner, may try and get away with it.

As previously, I shall say whether plants dislike lime and therefore must be in a lime-free scree and also whether some shade during part of the day is desirable unless you are prepared for much watering in hot dry weather, or happen to live in a part of the country where there is plenty of rain or the nights are cool with frequent dews. This explains, I hope, why I cannot tell you exactly what you must do, but only hint; you must use your head!

To obtain some of these plants will give you all the excitement of a Treasure Hunt searching catalogues on a winter evening.

We have seen some of the very pretty **Aethionemas** in both the preceding chapters. *Aethionema oppositifolium* is very different from the ones already mentioned, as it makes little tufts of grey oval leaves and the lavender-pink flowers really sit on the tuft. This is from the Lebanon. *A.iberideum* is a wee bit taller with white flowers.

The **Androsace** also has its scree species. *Androsace hedreantha*, from the Balkans, has 2-in. tufts of green and has plenty of bright, reddish violet flowers very little taller; it dislikes lime. *A.jacquemontii*, a charming Himalayan, is like a miniature *A.sarmentosa*, with heads of blue-pink flowers on 2-in. stems; *A.mucronifolia* is equally small but the rosettes are green and the flowers pale pink. *A.sempervivoides* is perhaps, as the name suggests, like a little green sempervivum or house leek, bright pink on 2-in. stems. *A.villosa* has very small hairy rosettes on which the white red-eyed flowers sit; it is said to be fragrant but I have never been able to get my nose near enough to test this; *A.v.arachnoidea* is hairier still.

Antennaria dioica minima makes a tiny, silver mat. It does not really require a scree but it is apt to get lost anywhere else, and its silvery leaves are attractive there.

The same remark applies to the little **Aquilegias:** *A.akitensis* and its variety *kurilensis*, *bertolonii*, *discolor* and *scopulorum*, all in some shade of blue or blue and white, and the last has in addition bluish green leaves.

There are even some dwarf **Arabis** that are appropriate to the scree, such as the pink *A.blepharophylla*, which you may let seed where it will, and *A.kellereri*, white on green cushions.

Arenaria ledebouriana is one of the rarer arenarias but it is very charming, because it makes tufts like a dwarf grey-green heather and the white flowers are on 3–4-in. stems little thicker than a hair.

There is a treasure in the **Woodruffs** that makes tufts of silvery woolly leaves and the little trumpet shaped pink flowers are on short spikes, the whole plant not more than 3 ins. high. Sometimes it is called *Asperula arcadiensis*, sometimes *A.suberosa*. They are not the same plant but are so for garden purposes, the difference being botanical. Both come from Greece and, unless on a wall or similar position, must be covered with a glass in the winter as they hate winter wet. Sometimes sparrows think the woolly shoots make an excellent lining for a nest, so beware. Summer flowering. For other Woodruffs, see Chapters 7 and 8.

Some years ago *Boykinia jamesii* came from Pike's Peak, Colorado, with a great flourish of trumpets that would be justified if it bore its cherry-red flowers more freely; the scree is the best hope for this. It makes a 2-in. tuft of little, scalloped leaves and the whole thing is only about 3 ins. tall. I have not yet been staggered by the amount of blossom. It is said not to like lime but with me, in a limy gravel scree, it has shown no objection.

The scree **Campanulas** are among the best of the scree plants. *C.allionii* runs about with little rosettes of green or grey appearing among the stones and then from these in early summer astonishingly large Canterbury bells 1–1½ ins. long appear. They may be deep purple, dark or pale lavender, blue-pink or white, but the last two are very rare.

C.arvatica (*acutangula*) from Spain resembles it only in running about; the bright green leaves are very small and the large deep violet stars come on 2-in. stems. There is a white form equally lovely and a deeper coloured form called Bevan's variety.

C.rotarvatica is a hybrid of this with one of the Harebells and, instead of stars, it has little upright purple bells, a wonderful, vigorous little plant in July–August.

C.autraniana from the Caucasus is rather astonishing, as the rich purple bells are so large and yet are only 1-2 ins. above the leaves on thready stems.

Those just mentioned flower in full summer, but the Japanese *C.pilosa*, which seems to have attracted to itself the word *superba*, comes in May; it makes a running mat on which sit the almost blue upright bells, of good size.

C.raineri is a gem from the Italian mountains, this also runs about and the 1-in. clear china-blue cups almost sit on the ground, waiting until July to do so.

However small the scree, I do not think anyone should omit any of these campanulas. For other campanulas, see Chapters 7 and 8.

The stems of the **Cyananthus,** cousins of the campanulas, clothed with small leaves, lie flat on the ground and the whole spread may be 12 ins.; they come from a tap root and that is the reason they like the scree with its very perfect drainage. The one usually seen is *C.lobatus*, which has a large purple blue flower at the end of each stem, and *C.l.insignis* is almost the same. I think these really do dislike lime.

C.microphyllus has very small leaves and the stems end with a flower like a periwinkle and this, in my experience, does not object to lime. All flower in late summer.

There are several little **Pinks (*Dianthus*)** which are best in the scree as they are seldom more than 2-3 ins. across and the flower stems are equally small. They are all pink and there is no point in describing each one, just try *D.freynii*, *haematocalyx*, *microlepis*, *musalae*, *scardicus pumilus* and *simulans* or any of these you can get hold of. You should like them.

The **Douglasias** may be called the America androsaces except for one European member, *D.vitaliana*. In the mountains its grey mats are golden yellow with flower which makes everyone anxious to grow it. Unfortunately it seldom flowers as freely in cultivation; free flowering forms are sometimes offered but I doubt them, it's just luck, but try the scree.

On the other hand the American *D.laevigata* is a free flowering plant with crimson flowers on mats of glossy green; it does not appear to like lime nor full sun, and in the mountains of

Oregon and Washington the best plants are said to be on north facing cliffs; try it in half-shade here.

I promised earlier that the best *Edraianthus* would come here. *E.pumilio* is a 2-in. mound of very narrow silvery leaves with, in May, a mass of upright lavender bells; I have had it seed about which is a very pleasant thing.

E.serpyllifolius, when it does appear in catalogues, is usually offered in the *major* form; this is certainly a worth-while plant, completely prostrate, deep green and covered with large, brilliant purple bells in May, but alas, it is said to be dying out because it does not set seed and therefore can be propagated only from cuttings.

But why, oh why, do nurserymen not grow *E.serpyllifolius* itself? The bells are the same colour or almost so, though not so large, but it does set seed, which is the best method of propagation and possibly from this another and vigorous *major* may once again appear, as it did for Reginald Farrer.

The best **Erigerons,** little brothers of the popular herbaceous border plants, are small tufted plants with quite good-sized daisies. They will grow in the rock garden but, being so small and neat, are better in the scree, the stems being usually only 2–3 ins., except in the mauve *E.simplex* which, curiously enough, in my gravel scree is 10 ins. tall and in the rock garden 6 ins. *E.aureus* is deep yellow. *E.flettii* which, like *E.simplex*, flowers for months, and *E.radicatus* are white, but *E.leiomerus* and *trifidus*, lavender; all from North America.

One of the Buckwheats, *Eriogonum ovalifolium,* is a white mat, hardly rising at all from the ground, and the little rounded heads are white or white and pink; a plant much to be cherished and always, yes always, covered with a glass in winter.

The one little **Erodium,** or Heron's Bill, for the scree is *E.chamaedryoides (reichardii)* white, pink veined, pink in the variety roseum. The whole plant – leaves and all – is only about 1 in. high. There is a double form of the latter which I don't like, you may. *Erodium corsicum*, pink, is sometimes offered but it is not reliably hardy, which is to be expected, as it grows on

Gentiana verna

Primula rosea

The author's rock beds 1 and 2

(see pages 24 and 25)

Small scree in the author's bed 4

Part of a rock pavement

A dry wall in the author's garden

Lewisia hybrids at Bodnant Gardens

Onosma albo-roseum

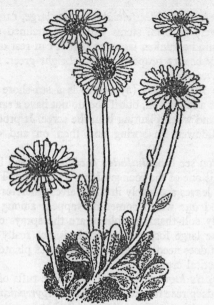

Fig. 14. *Erigeron flettii*

cliffs near the sea in Corsica, where I have seen it, and also in Sardinia. For other Heron's Bills, see the previous chapter.

Geum reptans, with feathery leaves and large golden flowers in summer, is the best of the geums but not the easiest; it needs or prefers a lime-free scree and if happy makes runners like a strawberry.

The **Globularias** I described in the last chapter. *G.incanescens* is a perfect scree plant of only 1 in., with little round balls of blue in June–July.

An 'everlasting' for the scree is *Helichrysum milfordae* (*marginatum*), a rather new plant, forming intense silver mats on which are scattered the crimson-budded, white, everlasting flowers; it appears to flower more freely if glass-covered in the winter.

F

Melandrium or *Silene elizabethae* has large, carmine-rose, clarkia flowers on 6-in. stems which are inclined to flop, so plant it behind a sunken stone so that it can rest on this and show off its beauty properly; it has bright green rosettes of pointed leaves.

Morisia monanthos (*hypogaea*) is a sea-shore plant and really wants a sandy soil, but if you do not have a sand bed use plenty of sand when planting it in the scree. It produces little yellow wallflowers in spring and then on and off during summer.

If ever you see **Omphalodes luciliae** you will be eager to grow it; it is one of the rock gardener's treasures. The tufts of blue-green leaves are lovely in themselves; therefore shun the green-leaved one which sometimes appear among seedlings. More lovely still than the foliage are the sprays of sky-blue flowers, like large forget-me-nots. It is not really a difficult plant but it does need a glass in winter unless planted in a wall or some vertical crevice.

Petrocoptis lagascae (*Silene*) has loose tufts of blue-grey leaves and deep rose flowers in summer. *P.pyrenaica* with paler flowers is sometimes offered; it is not quite so good a plant but has a certain charm and flowers freely.

Although they will grow on the rock garden, the smallest **Phloxes** such as *P.caespitosa*, *diffusa*, and *hoodii* are just as good or even better in the scree.

Phyteuma comosum from the Tyrol is one of the most astonishing plants you are likely to grow. It makes a rosette of dark holly-like leaves and in the centre in June–July there appears a head of little soda-bottles (the old kind which you may never have seen, pointed at the bottom), pale lilac with a deep-purple tip. Unfortunately slugs love it passionately.

Sometimes one or other of the most choice American Jacob's ladders or **Polemoniums** are offered and they are choice indeed. All have ferny foliage, dark or light green, which has a peculiar smell that some people liken to beer (good old beer, not like the present wish-wash), and eventually make clumps 1 ft across. Above these rise the flowering stem at about 10–12 ins. with heads of twenty or more 1-in.-long trumpets, in *Polemonium confertum* rich blue, *P.lanatum humile*, pale blue, *P.mellitum*, white or cream. *P.viscosum*, also blue, is a dwarfer *P.confertum*. They first flower in spring and then on and off during the summer. As much sun as possible for these.

If *Potentilla nitida* refuses to do its stuff in the rock garden, try it in the scree.

There may be an ugly buttercup here and there but certainly not among the dwarf ones, best in the scree. All have ¾-in. white buttercup flowers and neat tufted foliage. *Ranunculus alpestris* and *crenatus* are as good as any; watch the watering of these in dry weather. For other cultivated buttercups, see the previous chapter.

A scree which is not in full sun all day, preferably shaded in the afternoon when the heat is greatest, is a good place for what are known as the **Kabschia Saxifrages**. These all make cushions of small, spiny or flat-leaved rosettes, grey or green, which are covered with rounded or star-shaped flowers anything from ½ to 1 in. across on 1-in. stems in late winter or spring.

Some are plants which grow in the wild but a great number have been raised in gardens and when I tell you that my list of those in cultivation totals up to 95 you will, probably, be pleased to hear that I intend to give only a reasonable selection for the ordinary rock gardener; if you become a collector of these admittedly valuable plants, I will help you to find others. My selection is of those which I think everyone should try to grow, but someone else might choose an equally good one.

An important matter in cultivating these plants is to top dress them regularly after flowering with a gritty mixture of sand and loam and a little leaf-mould if you have it, otherwise the cushions may get hollow, in which case they suffer from sunburn. The following will, if happy, eventually make mats up to 1 ft across and might equally well be planted in the rock garden:

S.apiculata primrose, *a.alba*, white, *elizabethae*, pale yellow, *haagii* gold, L. G. Godseff, lemon, Primrose Bee, yellow.

Of the following more choice Kabschias, you will be lucky if you get healthy mounds bigger than 6 ins. across in the open, but they are the cream:

S.amitie, pale lilac, *S.borisii*, pale yellow, all the *S.burserianas* you can get, Brookside, *crenata*, Gloria, His Majesty, Magna, *major* all white, *b.major lutea* and Valerie Finnis, yellow. Christine, bright pink, Cranbourne, rose lilac, Faldonside, yellow, Hocker Edge, lilac pink, *S.jenkinsae*,

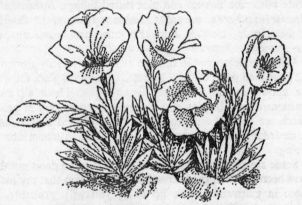

FIG. 15. *Saxifraga burseriana magna*

pink, *S.kestonensis*, white, *S.marginata coriophylla*, white, *S.marginata rocheliana*, white, Marie Louise, red buds, white flowers, *S.megaseaeflora*, rose, Mother of Pearl, pale pink, *S.paulinae*, pale yellow, *S.petraschii*, white, Queen Mother, rich pink.

Although there are about thirty of the group known as **Engleria Saxifrages**, they are by no means as important as the above; their rosettes are similar but a bit larger, the flower stems 2–4 ins. high and the beauty lies chiefly in the coloured bag (calyx) which surrounds the true flower, and the red hairs which often clothe the stem and stem leaves. I think that unless

you develop a passion for their quaintness, the following will
suffice:

S.grisebachii Wisley, crimson, *S.kellereri*, pink, and *S.poro-
phylla sibthorpiana*, purple. Give these the same conditions
as the Kabschias, but if necessary they will stand more sun.

I nearly forgot to mention **Saxifraga oppositifolia**, which
makes good-sized, real mats of green which in spring are
studded with flowers. There are several varieties all good
except the white. I have heard that there is in fact a good
white which I have not yet succeeded in obtaining, but the
ordinary form has rather poor starry flowers, whereas the
coloured ones have little cups sitting tight on the mats. Top
dressing as advised for the Kabschias is essential for these
also.

The usual form of *oppositifolia* is heather purple, but
S.o.latina has large pink flowers, *S.o.coccinea* is crimson,
S.o.splendens is the same or very similar and there are others; if
possible get W. A. Clark, which is a richly coloured variety of
our native plant.

Our native Moss Campion, **Silene acaulis**, and its brothers
in the Alps make iron-hard, green cushions smothered with
pink flowers in the spring, but this does not happen in the
garden. Fortunately there is a variety which flowers freely with
us, *S.acaulis excsapa*, and another which also does and is very
similar but the mats are loose, *S.elongata* (*S.acaulis saxatilis*).

You may be surprised to hear that there are two little
Spiraeas which are best in the scree; both American. I have
walked on mats of *S.caespitosa* in the Sierra Nevada which
were so hard that my boots made no impression on the minute
silvery-green rosettes and spikelets of fluffy white. *S.hender-
sonii* is a little taller, say 6 ins., and neither so hard nor tight but
with similar fluffy spikes of flower. I have seen it stated that it
dislikes lime, but it shows no signs of this on my tufa cliff.
These are sometimes called Petrophytum, but it makes no
difference to them, or us.

The **Thlaspis** should be grown because of their delightful
scent of heliotrope, although they may not be long-lived, but

they always leave some children to carry on. Both *T.limosellae-folium* and *rotundifolium* are little dark-green mounds with small lilac wallflowers in spring, the former having the least showy flowers but the strongest scent.

The tall and showy **Verbascums** or Mulleins of the herbaceous border have a dwarf brother in *Verbascum dumulosum*, a rather new plant from Turkey. Its leaves are covered with a dense felt of white hairs which set off the short spikes of large yellow flowers. A good plant, but I am not sure of its hardiness, as I have lost it once but am trying again. I have, however, seen it in the open as far north as Harrogate.

Strangely, in view of this, the spiny shrub-like *V.spinosum* from Greece is hardy here; the leaves are so small and grey that the yellow flower appears to be on bare branches. It wants it hot and dry.

I hope that the descriptions of the many good plants that require a scree will encourage you to make even a small one for trial, when you have got your hand in by growing the easier things. I do not mean that scree plants are difficult, but they do need, perhaps, a little more attention than the ordinary run and are well worth it.

Lastly, early autumn planting is desirable, say early to mid September, so that they get their roots going before winter. In planting shake away the bulk of the soil as otherwise you will make the scree too earthy. You may plant in early spring but then must water freely until they start to grow.

CHAPTER 10

PLANTS FOR MOIST BEDS

IN Chapter 5 I described the making of beds for growing those dwarf plants that require more moisture in their daily life than is available in the rock garden proper or any of the other variations. These are plants that at home grow in north-facing slopes, or in shady hollows on the mountain-side or in the open but still shaded places in woods, or in areas where there is a heavy rainfall or frequent wetting mists during their growing life.

To omit these would deprive you of growing many delightful plants and for me they are important inhabitants of the rock garden taken as a whole. When describing them I will mention their special wants if they have any, but do not forget that the farther north you go or the higher up or the wetter the district the less important is the matter of shade but not of soil.

Although a later chapter will deal with dwarf shrubs for the rock beds proper, I am including here, as the most suitable place, several dwarf shrubs that require the moist, peaty, leafy soil of which the bed is made and more or less shade.

Adonis brevistyla has flowers like white anemones with a blue back and ferny foliage; there are good and bad forms, so if possible see before buying. May flowering.

The **Andromedas** are neat, narrow-leaved shrubs with sweet, pink bells the size of large peas tucked in at the mouth, in spring. *A.polifolia compacta* (*minima*) and *A.p.grandiflora* (major) are from Japan and cannot stand lime.

What is known as the blue Himalayan buttercup is really an **Anemone**. It is *A.obtusi loba patula* and is often spoken of with awe. The colour is certainly good but to me the flowers are too small for the length of the prostrate stem, at the end of which

they appear in spring and sometimes autumn, but you are free
to disagree with me, as many do!

Arcterica nana is another of these lime-hating shrubs, only
4 ins. high with small white lily of the valley flowers; you have
to get close to it to admire it.

The little **Astilbes** do not mind lime provided there is
plenty of peat and leaf-mould in the bed. *Astilba crispa* Perkeo
has deep pink flowers in spikes and goes up to 8 ins., *A.chinensis
pumila*, lilac-rose, is 12 ins., as also may be those that I regard
as the best, *A.simplicifolia* and *A.s.rosea*, pale or deep pink.
A.glaberrima saxatilis is a quaint little pale pink pygmy only
2 ins. tall. All flower in late summer and are therefore doubly
useful.

Calceolaria tenella will creep over a moist rock just like
Arenaria balearica and has little calceolarias almost on the mat.
I am rather doubtful about its hardiness in cold places.

The **Cassiopes,** with white bells the size of good lily of the
valley flowers on stems like a Club Moss, some creeping, some
erect, are much grown by specialists, but it is worth trying one
or two, for they are so beautiful. They hate lime like poison, do
not like too much sun but if in full shade do not flower. My
greatest success was in a previous garden where on a north-
facing bed they had sun for only 3–4 hours a day and the soil
was leaf-mould mixed with lots of pieces of rotten wood. Try
C.lycopodioides from Japan, prostrate, *C.selaginoides*, erect,
from the Himalayas and the hybrid Muirhead.

There are several tiny New Zealand **Celmisias** which like
moist, peaty soil but not too much shade. The best are *C.argen-
tea*, which breaks out into little, white daisies on hard, silver
tufts, and the similar but slightly larger *C.sessiliflora. C.bellidi-
folia* differs in having a green rosette of leaves and in needing
full shade and plenty of water, as it grows near streams. All
these little fellows appear to dislike lime.

It is unusual for a succulent plant to like shade but *Cotyle-
don oppositifolia*, which you may also find under the
awkward name of *Chiastophyllum oppositifolium* and, to make
matters worse, as *C.simplicifolia*, does like shade and in this its

little drooping sprays of yellow flowers, like a miniature laburnum, are most attractive; try to place it between a couple of rocks so that the sprays do not flop on the ground.

The **Cortusas** are very like primulas, with rounded, hairy leaves and heads of drooping flowers some shade of crimson on 6-in. stems. *C.matthioli* is the one usually available and it does not mind lime; early summer. If any others become available they are all worth while for this season.

The ferny-leaved **Corydalis,** with little yellow tubes, is an easy and familiar cottager, but *C.cashmeriana* in the open in my garden is usually viewed with surprise because it is regarded as difficult. It is not really so if you put it in the right place and that is in full shade in the coldest spot you have in the garden. It has, in May, 4-in. sprays of an unusual electric blue only equalled in colour by some of the gentians, to which we shall come soon. It makes quantities of little tubers and is a great success in my limy soil mixed with moss-peat. It is far better out of doors than in a pot so do not be afraid of it, even if you are of the price.

Dutchman's Breeches, or *Dicentra cucullaria* pops up quickly in the spring with ferny leaves and flowers white, yellow topped, like little ancient harps or lockets. After flowering it dies away but is safe to appear again next year. *D.oregana* is larger and pinker, and prefers half-shade.

The **Dodecatheons,** or American shooting stars, with heads of cyclamen-shaped flowers, will flourish in this moist bed and do not be worried if they die down completely in July, for it is their nature. They are all much of a muchness with pink to lilac and crimson flowers, but *D.pauciflorum* Red Wings is outstanding for its brilliant crimson flowers and dwarf 6–8-in. habit, but get the others by all means.

Two dwarf Willow Herbs, or **Epilobiums,** should be planted in this bed because, as well as having attractive flowers, they produce them from June to autumn. *E.glabellum* is a green bush about 9–12 ins. tall, flowers white. *E.kai-koense,* which is much dwarfer, about 3 ins. with flower stems up to 6 ins., has bright pink flowers; these are large, as large as in the bigger *E.glabellum*, and the neater foliage is tinged with bronze. It is the choicer plant, not always long lived with me, but it is kind enough to leave a few children to carry on. You need not be afraid that these New Zealand willow herbs will be a curse, as some of the bigger ones are. For other Willow Herbs, see Chapter 8.

The Barrenworts or **Epimediums** are very accommodating plants for any half-shady place, but most of them are too vigorous and spreading to be good bedfellows for the other choice plants. You will appreciate this when you know that they are recommended for ground cover. *E.youngianum niveum* and *y.roseum* are the only ones small and safe enough to plant. If your bed is a fair size you might add at the back *E.x.warleyense* for the sake of its coppery-red flowers.

The **Gaultherias** are little shrubs grown for the beauty of their berries, not so much for the flowers; they like the same conditions as cassiopes, i.e., no lime, but are much easier to grow. *G.cuneata* has clusters of large pure white berries and will run about modestly if happy. On *G.miqueliana* the berries are white tinged pink and are said to be edible, but it will be some time before you can have a gaultheria tart. The first comes from China, the latter from Japan. I think these two will do for a start.

The lovely autumn flowering **Gentians** may come here, for they all require a leafy, peaty soil and, except in the north, half-shade and plenty of water in dry weather; moreover, excepting *Gentiana farreri*, they dislike lime, in fact *G.sino-ornata* so dislikes it that the mere sight of it is almost enough to kill it.

But if your soil is not very limy and you add extra moss-peat and leaf-mould (note that leaf-mould from trees on lime will be limy) you should try some of the hybrids that have *G.farreri* as one of the parents, such as Inverleith and Devonhall. The only one I can grow without any trickery, beside *G.farreri*, is Inverleith, but if you care to water with the expensive Seques-trene you may be able to grow *G.macauleyi* as well and some others.

All the plants are similar in growth – tufts of short, narrow, green leaves and huge upright trumpets on 3-in. prostrate stems. *G.farreri* is Cambridge blue with white throat, *G.sino-ornata*, deep blue, *G.* Inverleith, deep blue, Devonhall, pale blue, tubby flowers.

There is a host of hybrids and seeding varieties for those with suitable soil, varying in colour from pale to dark blue and long or short trumpets, and they make such a wonderful show from August into the autumn that you should try all you can afford. Not being able to grow most of these is the chief disadvantage of a limy soil.

It is curious that the New Zealand gentians (the others are Chinese or Tibetan), all have upward-facing white cups with contrasting black stems; the ones usually available are *G.bellidi-folia* and *G.saxosa*, the latter being the smaller; both flower in late summer. They do not appear to have quite the same horror of lime as most of the Chinese. For other gentians, see Chapters 7 and 8.

The **Haberleas** from Bulgaria have a really aristocratic air possibly because they are the relics of an ancient flora. There are only two species, both of which have rosettes of somewhat hairy, deep green leaves which in time make large clumps. Both *H.rhodopensis* and *H.ferdinandi-coburgi* bear lipped, lavender flowers with yellow throats on top of a short stem in May, those of the latter being more numerous, 6–8 against 2–3 and larger; they are very charming and are often likened to a small greenhouse streptocarpus or gloxinia.

As they are cliff or boulder crevice dwellers, haberleas dis-like having their rosettes resting on the damp ground, so in planting surround them with good sized pieces of rock. If the weather is dry and they are not watered, the leaves shrivel and curl up but do not be alarmed, they revive again with rain or watering.

The **Hepaticas** are really anemones and you may find them under either name in catalogues. They are very lovely and dwarf, flower in late winter or early spring and do not mind, in fact I think prefer, lime. They do, however, take time to establish, so do not expect the best results the first season, but they will go on more or less for ever, and if you attain good clumps do not attempt to divide them, even for your best friend.

Of *Hepatica triloba* there are single blue, pink and white forms and double pink and a rather rare double blue. The most outstanding plant of the lot is the hybrid *H.media ballardii*, with larger flowers of a striking lavender blue. *H.transsilvanica* is larger in flower and leaves than *H.triloba* and the only variety offered has light lilac flowers. This comes from Roumania, but *H.triloba* stretches right across the world from France to Russia, China, Japan and North America.

Houstonia, or Bluets, so called because of its small blue stars, is a frail, dainty little 3-in. plant from the USA which should not be put near anything big, it is so small that otherwise it may be smothered. The variety Fred Millard is deeper in colour.

Jeffersonia dubia from Manchuria is one of the treasures for the spring. The 1-in. flowers are true, clear, lavender and normally open just as the young bronze-tinted leaves are showing; if, however, it suffers a check from drought or night frost, the leaves will outgrow the flowers, which are then completely hidden and its great beauty is lost. In one place in my garden it behaves as it should, in another it does not and must be moved. The good spot is colder than the other and this may make it more like its home in Manchuria.

For lime-free soil the **Leiophyllums** are easy and charming little shrubs with pink buds and white flowers in May; *L.buxifolium* or any of its varieties are worth while.

Most of the **Meconopsis** are too tall for this bed, except Farrer's Harebell Poppy, *M.quintuplinervia*. This makes slowly spreading mats of hairy leaves and the nodding, pale blue flowers are on 12-in. stems in late spring; it can stand lime, but there is a tendency for meconopsis blues to become pinker in limy soil.

Nierembergia rivularis, if happy, can be rather too much of a spreader, so watch it. The pure white, upright bells almost sit on the mats of green leaves in summer, but if it spreads too much you can always dig up a piece to give to friends; it is too good a plant to give to enemies.

Very different from *Omphalodes luciliae* in its likes is **Omphalodes cappadocica**, as it loves shade and moisture. It is a larger plant, but not too large, and the sprays of flowers in spring are like large Forget-me-nots and the same true blue. It often seeds about reasonably.

The **Ourisias**, with penstemon-like flowers, are not subshrubby like the penstemons. The majority of those in cultivation come from New Zealand and have white flowers; the exception, *O.elegans* (*coccinea*), with scarlet blooms, comes from Chile. *O.elegans* makes running tufts and the scarlet tubular flowers are on 6-in. stems about June. *O.macrocarpa* and *macrophylla* are very similar with largish, deep-green leaves on thick stems which run about and root into the soil. The large, white-lipped flowers are numerous on the top of anything up to 12-in. stems; very handsome plants.

As far as my experience goes, all except *elegans* dislike lime and they all need at least half-shade.

Pernettya tasmanica is a tiny creeping evergreen grown for its large red berries; not for lime and doubtfully hardy but well worth a trial.

The **Phyllodoces** are little evergreen shrubs and are lime haters like the cassiopes but very much easier to grow. To produce freely their bell-shaped flowers on the tiny leaved shrubs, some but not too much sun is necessary. The best are *P.empetriformis*, rose, *P.nipponica*, white, and *P.tsugaefolia*, similar. These are 6–12 ins. tall and flower in late spring. You may see offered *P.aluetica* and *glanduliflora*, but these are for collectors, the flowers being officially 'chartreuse green', which means really a greenish yellow.

A phyllodoce is one of the parents of a pretty hybrid named **Phyllothamus erectus**, also a lime hater. It is a heath-like evergreen shrublet with bunches of pink flowers at the end of 6–8-in. stems, and well worth a trial, being comparatively easy.

Polygala chamaebuxus has the curious vernacular name

of Bastard Box because of the shape of its evergreen leaves. Its
varieties *grandiflora* and *rhodoptera*, although wanting shade
and peaty soil, do not object to lime, but they must be moist.
The flowers are winged like pea-flowers and in the first are
cream and yellow and in the other two crimson and yellow.
P.chamaebuxus is common in the woods of European mountains. *P.vayredae* from Spain is very similar in flower to
P.c.rhodoptera but the leaves are not box-like.

Many lovely **Primulas** will like this moist bed, but I do not
propose to tell you about those stately 2-ft naiads that like it
even wetter, as our bed is not a bog and 2 ft is taller than is
suitable for the small rock garden. Nor shall I tell you of what
are known as the *petiolarids* which, beautiful as they are, are
very much plants for the specialist and never perfectly happy
except in the north and Scotland; you can put a lot of money
down the drain in trying them unless you live in a district
where other rock gardeners grow them with success. The
following are the ones for us.

P.clarkei is a lovely spring-flowering miniature, having mats
of leaves flat on the ground and clear rose-pink flowers on 2-in.
stems just as the leaves are appearing. It must be divided at
least every two years but it is worth it and needs full shade.

P.frondosa is like an enlarged edition of our native Bird's
Eye primrose, *P.farinosa*, with flowers in mauve pink; it also
requires frequent division if you are to keep it going as a clump,
as it is very apt to 'go off' in the winter.

The sweet-scented *P.involucrata*, although liking the wettest
corner, should also be tried, as the white, lavender-tinted
flowers at the top of an 8-in. stem in early summer and the tuft
of small green leaves make a charming plant.

Lastly, not only for the water's edge but also in any moist
place, you must not omit *P.rosea*, of which Delight is the
deepest coloured among many other beautiful forms. It was one
of the first rock plants I bought over sixty years ago. It flowers
about April.

The **Ramondas** are cousins of the haberleas and like similar
conditions, that is to say shade, a moist soil and to be planted

between stones so that their leaves do not rest on damp earth; like haberleas the leaves shrivel if they get dry but recover again with rain. *R.myconi* (*pyrenaica*) is a wonderful sight in the Pyrenees, the hairy-leaved rosettes line rock crevices and are covered with large blue-lilac flowers on 3-in. stems; there are rare pink and white varieties but not one exceeds the beauty of the type.

Rhodothamnus chamaecistus is one of the few heath family shrubs which will tolerate lime as it grows on limestone mountains, but in peaty, leaf-mouldy soil. The rose-pink, saucer-shaped (not bell) flowers come in late spring.

The **Schizocodons** are Japanese woodlanders and are among the choicest plants for this bed in half-shade and no lime. They are evergreen and both the young and the autumn foliage are tinted red; the exquisite flowers are fringed, pink bells of the greatest daintiness. Very small plants are difficult to get going, so it is always worth while paying more for a decent-sized one. All the plants offered are varieties of *S.soldanelloides* and the easiest is *magnus* (or *macrophyllus*), but not the most beautiful.

The same remarks apply to the even more lovely **Shortias**, the best of which come from Japan but the easiest is *S.galaci-folia* from North America. I suggest you do not rush to buy either schizocodons or shortias until you have acquired some skill and preferably consulted other rock gardeners in your locality who happen to grow them.

The **Soldanellas** also bear delightful, fringed, hanging bells in shades of lavender blue on thread-like 2-3-in. stems over mats of small rounded green leaves. In a moist peaty soil they do not object to lime, they make their buds in the autumn and slugs are very fond of these; if you have no slugs and still they do not produce flowers, try covering with a piece of glass a few inches above, during the winter. *S.alpina, montana, pusilla* and *villosa* are those usually offered; the last, with pink hairs in the flower stems, is usually the easiest and most likely to flower freely; try this first.

Only one **Spiraea** is suitable for this bed. It is *S.pectinata*, sometimes called Luetkea; this looks more like a mossy saxi-frage than a spiraea except that the white flowers are in fluffy heads. No lime, please.

Strange as it may seem, there is one **Sedum** which, although it has fleshy leaves, likes moisture but not full shade. It is *S.pulchellum* with rosy-purple flowers on coxcombs in late summer, and very effective then.

Tanakaea radicans from Japan also has little sprays of white like a spiraea in summer, but the leaves are toothed and fleshy. I am doubtful about lime for this.

The smallest and the largest flowered **Thalictrums** both like some shade and moisture. The smallest, only 3 ins. tall, is *T.kiusianum* from Japan; it has fern-like foliage and from June to autumn gives us little fluffy heads of pinkish flowers. The largest, with lavender flowers 1 in. across, is *T.diffusiflorum* with foliage exactly like a maidenhair fern. It is taller than any other plants I have recommended but so dainty that it does not seem out of place; it is usually stated to be 2–3 ft high, but my plants never exceed 18 ins. Neither objects to lime. This is a China-man.

The **Tiarella** usually seen, *T.cordifolia*, is apt to be too invasive for a small bed (it is, in fact, often recommended as a 'ground cover' plant), so it is better to choose *T.wherryi*, which has similar spikes of fluffy white or pinkish flowers; it is a bit taller, say about 12 ins., but will not smother other things and it flowers from the summer until the autumn and in this respect also beats *T.cordifolia*.

There are two little Globe-flowers or **trollius** with bright yellow flowers that are almost flat when open, not globes, which will like the dampest place, but they do not need a bog like our own native Marsh Marigold does. They are about 6 ins. tall and are *T.acaulis* and *T.pumilus*; both are Himalayan.

CHAPTER II

DWARF SHRUBS

IN this chapter I am dealing with three classes of shrubs:
those which will grow in the ordinary rock garden soil in sun
or half-shade, those that require a lime-free soil, sandy, loamy,
or peaty, under the same conditions, which I have not dealt
with in the previous chapter, and finally the dwarf conifers.

A few of these dwarfs dotted about here and there give a
good effect and also protect the smaller plants from wind and
give some plants that little bit of shade for which they are grate-
ful. They can be planted at the same time as the rock plants,
but the more usual time is October or April for those that are
evergreen and November or March for those that are deci-
duous, that is to say, lose their leaves in winter.

The naming of the dwarf conifers, which seldom or never
bear cones, is confused, so I give those that occur in the catalogues but cannot guarantee them as always correct. You
could, if you felt inclined, plant a whole rock bed with these
various dwarfs; it would be interesting but I have not seen it
done.

For Ordinary Rock Garden Soil

One of the first shrubs to try is **Alyssum spinosum
roseum**, which, although it is only 9 in. high, can spread 2 ft
or more. The leaves are small and grey and all the growths are
moderately spiny, particularly when old. The little heads of
flower appear in May–June and completely cover the plant.
There are good and bad forms, some so pale as hardly to justify

the word *roseum*, but a good one is a most attractive bush. A native of Southern Europe, it loves a dry place.

I remember seeing masses of the spiny **Anthyllis hermanniae** on a hill-top in Corsica, smothered with little yellow pea-flowers, the back of some being red, but the one in cultivation as far as I know is yellow, though it goes reddish inside as it fades. If grown as it should be, in full sun, it is not likely to exceed 18 ins. and as much across. It does not like a cold spot and although quite hardy should receive some protection the first winter after planting. Flowers in June–July.

There are a number of dwarf **Barberries**, most of them evergreen and with yellow to orange flowers, often crimson in the bud. *Berberis buxifolia nana* makes an evergreen 1-ft mound attraction in the winter, but, when I had it, it did not flower freely. *B.darwinii* is probably known to most of you, but the variety *prostrata* is the one for the rock garden and it flowers as freely as its big brother in late spring. The following you may find as varieties of *B.irwinii* or *stenophylla*, the name makes no difference to their beauty and usefulness.

B.corallina compacta, *gracilis nana* and *picturata*, with pinkish young growths, are all about 1 ft tall.

A very dwarf variety, 6 ins. or so, of the South American *B.empetrifolia* with yellow flowers has recently come on the market and will be an acquisition.

Of the hybrid *B.stenophylla* itself there are two dwarf varieties – *autumnalis*, which flowers in spring and autumn, and *semperflorens*, which can eventually reach 3 ft but it takes a long time to do so.

Not many dwarfs give us autumn colour but the red-leaved plant with the awkward name of *B.thunbergii atropurpurea nana* (you need a large label for this) turns brilliant scarlet.

As far as I can ascertain there is only one dwarf of those barberries which lose their leaves in winter and which we cultivate for autumn colour and the beauty of their berries and this is *B.wilsonae globosa*, but this does not berry freely.

Before 1962–3 one could have recommended a number of dwarf **Cistus,** the true Rock Roses, for the rock garden but that winter played havoc with those in the open even in the South West; you might try the fairly hardy large-flowered dwarf Silver Pink and get away with it; I did not!

Although their May-like flowers have a certain attraction, the dwarf **Cotoneasters** are grown for their red or scarlet berries. The best for your purpose are:

C. adpressa, which loses its leaves in autumn after they have first gone scarlet; it can spread but may be cut back if necessary. *C.congesta* (*microphylla glacialis*), however, is really compact. *C.dammeri* is sometimes recommended but I found its long growth inclined to spread too far. On the other hand, *C.microphylla thymifolia* is a perfect rock garden shrub.

There are several **Brooms** that are suitable for the rock garden. If you have room, I mean for something that will probably be 2 ft across eventually, it is worth planting the golden broom *Cytisus beanii* or even *C.kewensis*, which is cream; but where space is limited plant *C.ardoini*, about 6 ins. tall with bright yellow flowers, from the Maritime Alps, and *C.demissus*, from Greece, which is a mat-former and on this appear large yellow flowers tinged brown at the base. In catalogues you may see *hirsutus* stuck in front of or behind *demissus*, but take no notice of this; if the word *demissus* is used, that is the plant you want.

C.decumbens is even more of a mat-former with extremely small leaves and gold pea-flowers. All the brooms flower in late spring or early summer. See also under Genista, which is also a broom.

The **Daphnes** have a bad name with some people because bushes of the mezereon (*Daphne mezereum*) are apt to die suddenly without apparent cause, but I have found them long lived, particularly in dry soils and they do not object to lime, in fact I think they prefer it.

There are, however, several other Daphnes, of great beauty. They are evergreen and relatively slow growing, so that in the small garden they need never be moved, which they dislike. Those that follow are all desirable.

D.arbuscula from Hungary is the neatest with small leaves

and rose-pink scented flowers; it is 6 ins. tall and in years may be 12 ins. across.

D.cneorum eximia is the best form of *D.cneorum*, with heads of deep pink, crimson budded, sweet-scented flowers in May. It wants room as, if happy, it will soon be 3 ft across; it can be cut back but it is a shame to do so and sometimes daphnes resent this very much, so give it a place where there is room for it to expand to its heart's content.

D.collina, with similar, sweet-scented flowers but larger leaves, gets up to 9 ins. or 1 ft; doubt has been cast on its hardiness but it did not suffer with me in the Midlands in 1962–3, although it comes from the Mediterranean region.

D.retusa and *tangutica* are very similar Chinamen, making rounded bushes eventually 1 ft tall and 1½ ft across but this takes some time; the clusters of scented flowers are white inside, deep crimson without. *D.tangutica* grows more rapidly and flowers sooner than *D.retusa* and therefore the small plant you are likely to obtain is preferably the former, and it is unfortunate that it is the latter which is more generally offered – why I do not know as both are raised easily from seed.

Euryops evansii is a newcomer from South Africa and surprisingly hardy. The shoots, with leaves of true silver, end in summer with clear yellow marguerites on short stems; eventually it makes a shrub 1 ft or more across about 9 ins. tall. It dislikes intensely damp air or rather, if it gets this, it is liable to a fungus disease; therefore plant it in as high and dry a position as you can find and it will be lovely both in summer and winter.

Genistas, as most people know, are very like Brooms and equally useful, and only botanists can tell the difference. *G.delphinensis* is a dwarf *G.sagittalis*, in which the yellow pea-flowers appear on curious winged stems; it is better than the latter because it does not spread too much. *G.dalmatica* is the nearest you will get to having a dwarf gorse in the rock garden; it is 6 ins. tall and equally spiny. *G.pilosa* is quite prostrate and a good plant but in time likely to cover too much ground, so look out for the smaller *G.pilosa minor*.

Smallest of all, slow growing and with 3-in. erect shoots and yellow flowers at their ends, is *G.villarsii*; it is so small that it must have a select place in the sun.

The **Halimiums** might be called yellow cistus, and most of them are tender in the sense that 1962-3 finished many of them, but with me *H.alyssoides*, which has 1-in. clear yellow flowers, survived and so must be hardy; it is taller than the other shrubs I am talking about, say 2 ft, but it is so slender and airy that it can fit into a small rock garden easily, and the single yellow roses on grey bushes are attractive in June–July.

I have earlier mentioned those Sun Roses (**Helianthemum**) that are suitable for massed colour, but there are several real dwarfs that can be used among the rock plants; they are *Helianthemum alpestre*, quite prostrate with yellow flowers, and *H.lunulatum*, which makes a neat, rounded bush only a few inches high with yellow flowers having an orange spot at the base of each petal.

A shrubby and hardy **Helichrysum** is *H.selago* from New Zealand. It is a slow growing bush of whipcord branches and the little green leaves are edged with white, giving a charming effect. The everlasting flowers are white but the bush must be some size before these are produced.

Jasminum parkeri is in effect a yellow jasmine in the shape of a little bush; it is said to be hardy but I lost it in 1962-3, so it is wise in the colder parts to give it a warm, sunny place.

Most **Lavenders** are too large for the small garden but there are two which are only about 6 ins. high and which fit in perfectly, known as Baby Blue and Baby White; I prefer the former as white in a lavender never attracts me. If you have room for one somewhat taller, try the rich purple Hidcote which grows over 1 ft but may be clipped after flowering, as all of them may; or Munstead Dwarf, which is not quite so deep in colour. These, of course, flower in the summer.

The shrubby **Potentillas** are excellent, long flowering shrubs for the garden and all have flowers like single roses.

Several are suitable for the rock garden. *P. fruticosa beesii* has silver leaves and gold flowers. Longacre is similar but the leaves are green.

P. farreri prostrata is not entirely prostrate, as it may get up to 1 ft, but you can cut off the taller shoots; this has large 1½-in. golden flowers. Barnbarroch is prostrate with exquisite pale yellow flowers of the same size. *P. f. mandschurica* is really prostrate, small in flower but pure white.

Tangerine is about 1 ft tall, the colour being unique, not quite the colour of a tangerine, but it must be in partial shade as the colour fades quickly in sunlight.

If potentillas do get too big they can all be carefully trimmed in the spring.

One must have a plant of the dwarf **Almond** for spring flowers. The best undoubtedly is *Prunus tenella* Fire Hill (the dwarf Russian almond), with rosy crimson flowers and it is not so inclined to wander about and make a thicket as the ordinary one is.

I wish I could recommend a dwarf **Rosemary,** so that you could pinch its leaves when passing, but the only prostrate one is not hardy and that is all there is to it.

The dwarf **Willows** have a certain charm, both in their habit of growth and their little catkins, but I cannot claim that they make a great show. Three will probably be enough for you, so I suggest:

Salix boydii because it makes an aged looking tree of only a few inches high, quite Japanese in effect.

S. reticulata because it is prostrate and the deeply veined leaves are most attractive, and

S. retusa because the little unopened catkins are mahogany-red over the grey leaves.

S. boydii does not like lime, but the others do not seem to mind.

For a pure silver-grey effect nothing beats the dwarf Cotton Lavender, **Santolina incana nana,** the leaves of which have been justly described as giving a filigree effect; the flowers are yellow buttons of no great value. It needs full sun and can be clipped back as and as often as you like to keep a nice rounded bush about 1 ft tall.

Among the dwarf **Spiraeas,** *Spiraea bullata* is often seen and recommended, but to me its wrinkled puckered leaves make it look as if mauled by some insect, though the clusters of scarlet rose flowers are effective. *S.bumalda nana* Nyewoods is to me better, with flat heads of rosy flowers in July–August. My 1-ft bush, 2 ft across, has over 60 heads of flower at the time of writing, a really good plant. It tolerates lime but is better without it.

S.decumbens is more or less prostrate with sprays of white flowers, as also is *S.hacquetii*, but you do not need both; they run about underground and need a space of a foot or more, so be careful where you put them.

You may be surprised to hear that there is a little Mountain Ash, or **Sorbus,** but there is. It is *Sorbus reducta,* and a very choice plant too, running about very quietly and in time 1 ft across and 6 ins. or so tall; the berries are red. Give it plenty of sun.

The valuable shrubby **Veronicas** from New Zealand are now called Hebes, but fortunately most catalogues stick to the old name. Their habit is good and dwarf, the leaves are attractive and they flower freely, some extremely so in spring or summer, and they suffer no harm from trimming when desired. The starry flowers are in loose or tight spikes, white or pale or dark lavender-blue. I find them some of the most useful and attractive dwarf shrubs for the rock garden.

There are several to choose from. *V.albicans* is white on a mound of sea-green, *V.armstrongi* is a bronzy-gold whipcord bush and in this its main attraction lies, as it gives an entirely distinct effect. *V.* Bowles Hybrid is a neat shrub with spikes of mauve flowers. *V.buchananii* is a neat greyish bush with white flowers and *V.b.minor* is a perfect pet, only 2 ins. tall and, being so small, needs a select spot.

V. Carl Teschner is an excellent plant originally sent to me as a rooted cutting from New Zealand by the man of that name. It is a natural hybrid found by him. I have distributed it widely and it recently received an Award of Merit from the Royal Horticultural Society. On the mound of dark-green leaves spikes of violet flowers appear profusely in June and July.

V.pageana is the earliest to flower in April–May; the flowers are white and the grey leaves are edged with red when young.

In *V.pimelioides* the grey leaves are very small and dainty set off by the dark stems, and the loose bush it forms is covered with pale or dark violet-blue flowers. The variety *glauco-cae-rulea* is a more brilliant silver-grey.

There is a dwarf variety of *Viburnum fragrans* called *compactum*. I bought it when it first came out and never had a flower, but a piece I gave to a friend flowered freely on the top of a terrace. At 18 ins. high it is good when it does flower, but I cannot give you the recipe.

For Lime-Free Soil

Those who live on limy soils are unable to grow, with the exceptions mentioned, the shrubs which I will now describe unless they make up special beds raised to a foot above ground-level and have available rain-water for dry weather. There are so many plants that one can grow on lime that I do not myself think it worth the trouble the building and maintenance of such beds involves and I doubt whether the plants will ever look as happy as they do in places where the natural soil and water are lime-free; but it is for you to decide.

Apart from the soil being lime-free, these plants benefit from digging in some extra moss peat or leaf mould, particularly if very sandy or heavy and, if the latter, some gravel or chips as for the rock beds.

The Heather Family. What in England we call Ling (*Calluna vulgaris*) in which the flowers are not bells but divided into four, in Scotland is called heather, which is very confusing. There are numerous varieties and the problem is, how much room have you? Assuming that the answer is, not much, it is best to confine yourself to the small ones, as some grow up to 2 ft, and so those I shall mention will be about 6–9 ins.

I once, when on a suitable soil, made a collection of all the small varieties of heathers, both ling and bell, I could lay my hands on and a very interesting search it was. So here goes:

Calluna vulgaris alba aurea is worth growing for its yellow-tipped foliage as well as the white flowers. *C.v.alba rigida* spreads sideways although only 4 ins. upwards. County Wicklow is double and pink and 9 ins. tall.

C.v.foxii floribunda and *nana* both flower but *C.v.foxii* is flowerless. Mrs Ronald Gray is quite prostrate. These and *C.v.minima* and *C.v.minima* Smith's variety all have heather-purple flowers.

C.v.nana compacta makes little buns. Sister Anne has silvery foliage which goes red in winter and pink flowers; similar is The Pygmy, whereas Tom Thumb is an upright dwarf.

All the callunas or lings flower in August–September and are usually the heather of which you see purple miles on the moorlands if you visit them on your summer holiday. I was not able to find a dwarf form of the Irish Heather (*Daboecia polifolia*), so now we come to the true heathers or ericas and here we have a few that do not mind limy loams if a good proportion of moss-peat or leaf-mould is mixed with the soil.

These are the Winter Heather, *E.carnea* and its varieties, some of the *E.hybrida* forms and, strangely enough, *E.vagans* the Cornish Heath. Any of the *E.carnea* varieties are worth growing and they are all about 6 ins. tall and flower in winter-spring, that's what makes them so valuable. I like *E.c.aurea* because of its golden foliage, *E.c.* Cecilia, M. Beale, white, Eileen Porter, carmine, Ruby Glow, bright pink, and Springwood White, and there are many others.

The following varieties of *Erica hybrida* also do not object to lime; George Rendall, pink, and Silberschmelze (or Silver Beads), which goes up to a foot or so but is so good and white that it must be included.

Of the lime-haters there is the Dorset Heath *Erica ciliaris*, of which the only dwarf is *E.ciliaris hybrida*, having clusters of rosy pink at the end of the stems; if one corner of the garden is damper than other parts put it there.

The true Bell Heather is *Erica cinerea* and there are almost
too many from which to choose. The smallest are: *E.c.alba
minor*, *E.c.atrorubens*, bright red, *E.c.coccinea*, bright crimson,
Eden Valley, lilac pink, Golden Drop, with gold foliage, red in
winter, Mrs Dell, very dwarf, pink.

The Cross-leaved Heather, *E.tetralix* will stand a really
moist position; the flowers are in drooping clusters at the end
of the stems. Con Underwood, at 9 ins., is one of the best, with
crimson flowers and silver foliage; Mary Grace is bright pink
as also is *E.t.praegeri*, both 6 ins.

The Cornish heath, *E.vagans*, will grow on lime although I
know of none in Cornwall. There is only one dwarf variety,
E.vagans nana, with creamy-white flowers.

It will be seen from these notes that the numerous varieties
of the heaths differ a good deal in their needs, but one thing
they all share in common is love of an open situation in full sun.

For those with a suitable soil the dwarf **Rhododendrons** are
indispensable. In the south they like some shade during part of
the day but in the Midlands and North revel in full sun. Here
is a choice:

R.calostrotum bears large, magenta-crimson flowers and the
leaves are grey. *R.cephalanthum*, with pink heads of flower like
a daphne, is charming. *R.fastigiatum* is a beautiful hummock
without its lavender-purple flowers, as the leaves are blue-
green. In *R.hanceanum nanum* the little trumpet flowers are
pale yellow, but in *R.impeditum* blue-purple.

R.keleticum is a real mat-former, dotted with purple crimson
blossoms. *R.myrtilloides* is most attractive because of its plum-
coloured bells with a waxy bloom on the outside. *R.nitens* is also
very dwarf and, although its magenta pink is not the most
attractive colour, it flowers in June–July when the others have
finished.

R.pemakoense has large, mauve-pink blossoms and is very
good. *R.radicans* is another mat-maker with bright green
leaves and flat purple flowers. The lovely pink *R.racemosum*
must not be omitted, but get Forrest's dwarf as other varieties
can grow very large.

If you want something startling with large, waxy-red or deep pink bells, try the hybrids of *R. forrestii* (or *repens*), which itself rarely flowers freely, but Carmen, Little Bert and Treasure do. Yellow Hammer is taller up to $1\frac{1}{2}$ ft but its bright yellow bells make it worth growing.

It is quite feasible to devote a rock bed to dwarf rhododendrons only. They look well among the stones as they grow in the wild on rocky mountain sides, and appreciate snuggling up against them but these, of course, must not be limestone in any form.

Dwarf Conifers

A few dwarf conifers, the majority of which are evergreen, add something quite different to the little rock garden scene, but they should not be overdone. Some are so slow growing that they will never become too big; others, although no less attractive, may become too large in the course of years, and if this happens, rather than let the rock plants be smothered, it is best to scrap them and start again.

I find it quite impossible to put into plain words exactly what the different dwarfs are like; if you know what the forest cedars, cypress, firs, pines and junipers look like you will have some idea, but not a complete one, as some of the dwarfs have what is known as juvenile foliage, that is to say, like that of seedlings, which alters as the trees grow bigger.

Never having really made a study of them, I must admit that I cannot easily distinguish between the different cypress or the various firs, but I do know a pine when I see one. So you must take my word that the few I shall mention, of which I have had experience, are worth growing, and slow.

To learn more about them, look at them carefully at shows, in nurseries or in other gardens and always inquire their age and whether grafted or on their own roots. Except for the pines, *never* buy a grafted plant, for the chances are that, although you may think you are getting better value for your money, it will grow too fast and much too big. I shall mention the class to which the various plants belong so that we shall learn a bit more about them together.

The dwarf **Silver Fir** is *Abies balsamea hudsonia*, with dark green foliage, grey underneath; it will be years before it is 1 ft across.

The **Lawson Cypress** is *Chamaecyparis lawsoniana* and it is one of the False Cypress with flat branches. *C.l.nana* makes a bright-green globe. The best plants are the Japanese Cypress, which are little pygmy trees like balls of moss and slow growing: *Chamaecyparis obtusa caespitosa*, *C.o.juniperoides*, and *C.o.minima*, which are all much the same for garden effect. *C.pisifera nana* is blue-green and flat, but the one you must get is *C.p.squarrosa cyano-viridis* for its blue-green colour and, for a change, add the gold-tipped *C.p.nana aureo-variegata*.

Of the **Junipers**, one must have a specimen of the Noah's Ark tree, *Juniperus communis compressa*, to remind you of your children, that is if children have Noah's Arks these days.

Although one day a long way ahead it will be 2 ft tall, it is worth planting one of the **Japanese Cedars**, because its leaves are so arranged that it looks like a Club Moss, and these turn bronze in winter; this is *Cryptomeria japonica vilmoriniana*. I am not mentioning the dwarf form of the Cedar of Lebanon as it is very rare and very expensive.

However, you must have one **Spruce Fir**, and a grey-green mound-former with flat branches is *Picea mariana nana*.

A miniature **Scots Pine**, *Pinus sylvestris beauvronensis*, makes a perfect Japanese picture but it is expensive. The real pine of Japanese pictures and pottery is *P.parviflora*, which is very slow growing and in my previous garden I liked it better than the Scots Pine; it also is expensive but no miniature pine is cheap.

You have probably heard people talking of **Douglas Firs** in the National Forests and a really handsome dwarf is *Pseudotsuga glauca fletcheri*, but it is no good on chalk. When you are getting old it may be 2 ft tall, and then probably you will not wish to scrap it.

I think everybody can recognize the sombre **Yews**, so fre-

quently seen in churchyards, and there is one really nice little
miniature, *Taxus baccata pygmaea*, which you may like to try.
By the time you have planted this little lot, if you have room,
you will know enough about dwarf conifers to go on further if
you wish to do so, and other books must guide you as I am no
expert on these.

CHAPTER 12

PROPAGATION

BY SEED — BY CUTTINGS — BY DIVISION

By Seed

To start a collection of rock plants you will have to buy a few and beg some from your friends, but be careful that they do not give you any of those about which I have given a warning. If your pocket is not very deep and if you are prepared to take a little trouble you can build up quite a respectable collection by raising plants from seed – not all those I have talked about, because some do not set seed in this country and some, like many of the pinks, do not breed true. There is a tremendous lot of swapping among gardeners and propagation is the way for you to have plants to swap for things you want.

The first thing you need is a little patience, but then, if you do not have this you will never be a gardener – more likely a casualty on the roads.

Although you will see advertisements of various patent or plastic pots, I still prefer and recommend the clay; they are so much easier to manage in the matter of watering. I use almost entirely those of 3½-in. inside diameter. For soil, use John Innes Seed Compost; it is so much simpler than mixing one's own, and, being sterilized, it does not or should not produce weeds.

This compost does vary somewhat, depending on the maker, so, for rock plants generally, to every two pots of J.I. I add one pot of coarse sand, mixing thoroughly in a bucket and watering if the mixture is dry. The way to tell whether it is OK is to take a handful, clench, and then there should be a little mound of soil on the palm, and if, on just pressing with the finger, this mould falls to bits it is all right; if not it is too wet, and if it disintegrates on opening your hand it is too dry.

For peat and shade lovers I use one pot J.I., one pot damp moss-peat broken up, one pot coarse sand. For all the hundreds of plants I have raised from seed I have not beaten these mixtures.

Now for the procedure. If the pots are new, soak them in water for 5 minutes and let them dry, before use. At the bottom put a large piece of broken pot or better, a little square of per-forated zinc which you can cut from a piece with a tinsmith's snip; over this place a few pieces of smaller broken pot, or small pebbles, or stone chips and cover them with a layer of moss-peat to prevent the soil washing down into the drainage. Fill up with the soil mixture to within $\frac{1}{2}$ in. of the top and tap the pot on the bench to settle it.

Some packets you get will contain many more seeds than you can possibly want as plants and a couple of dozen seeds in the $3\frac{1}{2}$-in. pots is ample. If the seeds are large, space them out, press them into the soil with the bottom of another pot, cover with about $\frac{1}{4}$ in. of soil, press this down also and finish off with a thin layer of coarse sand; this is to prevent the soil being beaten down by rain or watering and the spattering of the seedlings with soil.

If the seed is small, scatter as evenly as you can over the sur-face, then cover with a little soil, not so much as for the big seeds, but finish off with sand, so that roughly you finish off $\frac{1}{4}$ in. below the rim.

Now what do you do ? Well, I plunge the pots up to the rim in builders' sand in the open in a place which does not get more than a few hours of sun a day. If you are in a dry place, it helps to plunge in moss-peat or a mixture of this and builders' sand. In dry weather these pots will need water every other day. I know that with the sand surface you cannot tell by looking whether the pot is dry or not, but with the well-drained mix-ture I have recommended you are not likely to over-water. Pots of seed of shade-lovers should be in as much shade as you can manage.

Now when the little plants begin to show, what to do with them? If this happens from March to September I leave the pots where they are, but if in October or any time up to the end of February (and some seeds are so very erratic they will come at odd times), I move the pots into a cold frame, and plunge as before, always, except in severe frost, leaving the lid of the frame open a trifle to let a little air in.

If you do not have a cold frame, a wooden box and a sheet of glass or a tent cloche will give just that bit of protection from battering rain which is required; or, simpler still, you may cover them in the original plunge bed with a cloche or two.

The ideal time to sow is September–October, but it is seldom that you will get the seeds before January–February, so sow in February–March if you have time but you can sow up to the end of May quite safely.

What I do next is this. As I said, I doubt whether you will require more than a dozen plants of any one thing; if there are more in the pot than that I pull some out with a pair of tweezers and this gives the dozen left room to grow bigger. Now the ideal is to transplant the remaining seedlings from out of the pots when they have made 3–4 little leaves but often, for one reason or another, this is not possible, though they must be moved if roots appear at the drainage hole. The seedlings will be too small to put at once in the rock garden, so you must 'prick' them out, as it is called, into boxes of any size, with drainage holes at the bottom covered with moss-peat, or into other pots, using the same mixture as before.

Alternatively, they can be transplanted into a little select nursery bed in half-shade. If your soil is very sandy, fork in some moss-peat or leaf-mould and a little better soil if possible; if on the heavy side or if it lies wet, add coarse sand and moss-peat to lighten it. In time you will get to know when soil is right by the feel much better than I can describe in words.

To get the seedlings out of the pots with as little damage as possible, let the pot get slightly on the dry side. I put mine in the potting shed for a day. Holding the pot on the slope, tap the edge of it on the bench and poke a finger through the drainage hole; this should loosen 'the ball' so that you can gently pull the pot away.

Then, on tapping the ball of soil, it should fall apart and the seedlings can be easily separated without damaging the roots. If the soil is too wet, leave the 'ball' on the bench until it is dry enough; trying to separate seedlings from wet soil is almost sure to tear the roots, which is as upsetting for the plants as a surgical operation may be on yourself.

Wherever you plant them, make the hole with a piece of wood or very narrow trowel, deep enough to take the full length of the roots. Water freely to start with and, if very hot, shade with newspaper or anything handy for a couple of weeks.

The plants should be big enough to put into their permanent positions in the rock garden in the autumn or following spring, but if they are still small then don't be in too much of a hurry but leave them another six months; they won't hurt. Seedlings require almost the care of children and they cannot shout if they want anything.

The following are easily raised from seed and, if the seed is good, should come up in a month or two. If these do not come up by the autumn I don't think it worth keeping the pots, but for slow seeds I keep the pots two years:

Achillea, aethionema, alyssum, aquilegia, arabis, arenaria, aster, most but not all campanulas, delphinium, dianthus, erigeron, erodium, erysimum, geranium, globularia, gypsophila, helianthemum, hutchinsia, hypericum, iberis, leontopodium, linum, lychnis, oenothera, papaver, petrocoptis, saponaria, scabiosa, sedum, sempervivum, silene, thalictrum, thlaspi, thymus, veronica, viola.

Others, unless sown in the autumn of their ripening year, may take up to twelve months before anything appears; get used to the easy ones first and then have a shot at the others, such as androsace, gentian, primula, ranunculus, saxifraga and any others not mentioned above.

By Cuttings

Apart from raising plants from seed, many can be raised at no expense by means of cuttings, some very easily. These cuttings may be taken from your own chosen plants or you may be able to get something new from a friend.

Wisley Pot for Cuttings

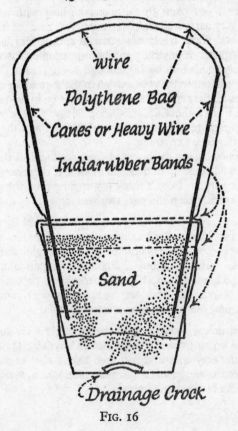

wire

Polythene Bag

Canes or Heavy Wire

Indiarubber Bands

Sand

Drainage Crock

FIG. 16

Cuttings give you a good sized plant quicker than seed. I do not suppose that, at the beginning of your interest in rock plants, you will possess a small frame used only for raising cuttings, so we will deal with the simple methods.

Pots can be used and should be filled with a mixture of half fine sand and half damp moss-peat thoroughly mixed. These, when the cuttings have been planted, can be covered with a polythene bag held up with bits of cane, as in Fig. 16, which makes them into little frames. Such pots are easy to manage, as they only require standing in water for a few minutes once a fortnight; most useful if you are away on holiday. Or the pots may be sunk in sand and covered with a box, of which you have knocked out the bottom and put in its place a piece of strong polythene sheet brought a little way down the sides and fixed with drawing pins (see Fig. 17).

Wooden Box for Cuttings

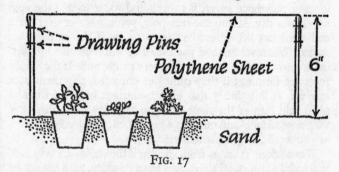

FIG. 17

Even simpler perhaps is to make a little bed of pure, fine sand or sand and peat and put a 2-lb. jam-jar over the cuttings after you have marked the space by pressing the jar a little way into the sand. Whichever system you use, the cuttings must be in as much shade as possible or, if not, paint whatever you use with a cream of flour and *cold* water, which gives excellent shade.

The best time to take most cuttings is July–August or even

September, except campanulas, phloxes, and some gentians, which must be taken from the new growths in spring. Cuttings, which must not be pieces showing a flower bud, need not be more than 2 ins. long, long cuttings having no advantage. Test if the shoot you intend taking is suitable by bending it and if it kinks it is too soft; if it bends easily without snapping it is about right. Plants with thick stems like erodium are always right if long enough to cut off with 2 ins.

To take the cutting, sever the stem immediately below a joint (or 'node') from which leaves are growing out with a sharp pair of scissors or sharp knife, trim off the leaves at the cut, and if the remaining leaves are too large for your box or pot, you may cut them in half. This form of propagating material is known as a nodal cutting. Make a slot in the damp sand or mixture with the knife blade, insert $\frac{1}{2}$ in. of the cutting and press the sand close up to it.

All you have to do then, after having put the pots under their glass or polythene cover, is to wait and water so that the sand never gets dry. If you use jam-pots, you can water over them and need not lift unless you want to see if the cuttings are rooted. Whatever method you use, they will show this by starting to grow, or you can test by a very gentle pull. If they resist roots are forming; if they come out unrooted, pop them back at once. It is unlikely that all the cuttings of any particular plant will root at the same time, so take out those that have with a wood label and nurse in a pot or bed, not closely covered, as you would a transplanted seedling.

When taking cuttings from shrubs, if the shoots are very soft, it is usual to pluck off short ones from an older, hard branch by a smart downward tug; this gives a little 'heel' of old wood. This is known as a heel cutting. Trim off the thin bit at the end and then go on as before. See Figs. 18 and 19 for this and other types of cutting.

Unless you get very interested, there is no point in taking cuttings of plants which can be 'divided' (see next section), because most of their growths have their own roots, or pieces with a root can be found – so-called Irishmen's cuttings!

Propagation — some cuttings

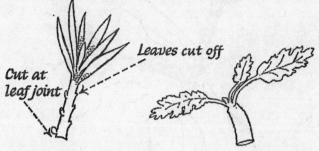

Cut at
leaf joint

Leaves cut off

Ordinary "nodal" cutting
just below leaf joint

Thick stem cutting

Cut off
tongue here

Heather cutting

Heel cutting

FIG. 18

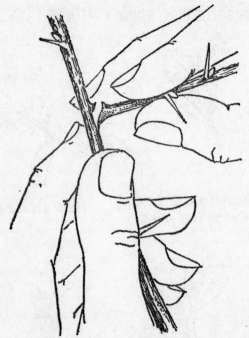

Taking a heel cutting

FIG. 19

One word of warning, do not mix cuttings of grey leaved or woolly plants with the others, as you must go slow with the watering of these, otherwise they may damp off. Cuttings of the following are all reasonably easy:

Achillea, aethionema, alyssum, *Androsace carnea*, *villosa*, anthemis, antirrhinum, arabis, arenaria, armeria, artemisia, asperula, calluna, campanula (in spring), chrysanthemum, crepis, cytisus, daphne (in May), cheiranthus;

Douglasia, dryas, *Edraianthus serpyllifolius*, epilobium,

erigeron, erica, erodium, erysimum, euryops, forsythia, genista, geranium, globularia, gypsophila, helianthemum, hippocrepis, hutchinsia, hypericum, iberis, jasminum, lavandula, linum except salsoloides, lithospermum, micromeria, moltkia;

Penstemon, phlox (in spring), polygala, *Potentilla fruticosa*, salvia, saponaria, satureia, santolina, schivereckia, sedum, senecio, silene, spiraea, tanacetum, tunica, verbascum, veronica (hebe), viola, zauschneria (in spring).

By Division

Many rock plants, like herbaceous ones, make roots at the base of each crown or shoot and obviously the easiest way to propagate these is by division. Any piece with a few roots, however small, should succeed but the smaller it is the more nursing you must give it.

Division is best done after mid-August into September and October. Water freely and, if planted directly in the rock garden, shade by covering with a pot if the sun is strong for about a fortnight. You may lift the whole clump and divide into as many pieces as you wish, or, if you know there are roots on some of the shoots, cut through the stem with a sharp knife and then dig up this piece carefully with a small fork.

Some plants make runners, particularly some androsaces; all you have to do then is, like strawberries, to put a small stone on the runner close to the newly formed little plant and, as soon as it is rooted, sever it from its parent and move it where you want it.

The following can usually be divided:

Acaena, achillea, *Androsace sarmentosa* (runners), antennaria, anthemis, ajuga, arabis, arenaria, artemisia, asperula except *A.suberosa*, aster, astilbe;
Calceolaria, campanulas that run, cerastium, ceratostigma, chrysogonum, cortusa;
Dodecatheon, doronicum;

Epilobium;

Gentiana acaulis, verna, and in spring only *G.farreri* and *sino-ornata* and their hybrids, *Geranium dalmaticum, lancastriense,* geum, *Globularia bellidifolia, Gypsophila cerastioides;*

Haberlea, *Helichrysum bellidioides, milfordae,* heliosperma, houstonia;

Iris just after flowering, jeffersonia;

Leontopodium, leucanthemum;

Mazus, *Meconopsis quintuplinervia, Mertensia echioides,* mimulus;

Nierembergia;

Omphalodes cappadocica, oxalis;

Parochetus, patrinia, penstemon (often make rooted growths but cuttings do better in the end), polygonum, potentilla, *Primula clarkei, frondosa, involucrata, rosea,* Prunella;

Ramonda, ranunculus, raoulia;

Scabiosa, most sedums, sempervivum, senecio, soldanella, solidago;

Tanakaea, *Thalictrum kiusianum,* tiarella, thymus, trollius, non-shrubby veronicas and sometimes branches of the hebes also root naturally;

Waldsteinia.

CHAPTER 13

PESTS AND DISEASES

I WISH I could say that rock plants are never attacked by pests or disease, but I cannot. If you found one or other of your plants being eaten or attacked and you depended on me to tell you and found no mention in the index you would rightly say you had been 'sold a pup'.

Now the worst pest is undoubtedly the slug and snail in one or other of their many varieties, as they will eat shoots, flowers, anything. As they breed so freely, you can never hope to rid your garden of every one, but they can be controlled, and much easier than in my youth, when I had to go round at night with a hat pin and a jug of salt water to finish them off.

The meta slug baits do kill them. I prefer the pellets or little macaronis as they stand up better to rain. You can scatter them about among your plants, particularly in tufted ones, merely as a precaution and if you see anything eaten and a trace of slime, put a pellet or two near by. If the weather is dry, it is possible to spray the whole rock garden with one of the liquid preparations, such as Slugit, and this is even more effective, and it does not harm seedlings. I use both.

Slugs and snails are particularly dangerous among seedlings, one of which is a very small meal to these terrors. I find that they love to hide on the side of plunged pots because they are damp and I spend a quiet time each Sunday morning lifting the pots and killing any I see; it has paid dividends. Sometimes you will find against the pot or on the sides of the hole clusters of what look like transparent Beecham's pills; these are their eggs, squash them at once. Slugs seem to like some plants more than others and I promise myself one day to make a list of these, but at nigh on eighty I shall have to hurry up. At the moment I can

only say that they love campanulas, pinks, edraianthus, primulas and violas.

Flowers and leaves may also be eaten by caterpillars in
season, so if you find no dead slug by your plant, search is the
thing and a squash the best remedy. Sometimes you will find
the growth eaten down to the ground level, or the plant flagging although not dry; this is probably due to the caterpillar of
the hart-and-dart and yellow underwing moths or cockchafer
grubs, which live underground. Forking gently round the plant
will usually bring them to the surface; if not, hunting at night
with a torch is the best way to find them. Forking in DDT
helps.

Sometimes, but rarely, green fly do attack rock plants, particularly the undersides of aquilegia leaves; a spray with Abol X
will finish these off and probably keep them off for the rest of
the season.

The minute red spider may attack some of the primulas. It
can be recognized by a yellow mottling of the leaves and a small
lens will show them on the underside; regular spraying with
Malathion is the only thing that I find effective.

If your garden is on new ground, you may be troubled with
wire-worm eating the roots; fork in Gamma BHC dust round
the roots; even better, because you can see the result, is to put a
stick in the top of a small carrot and bury this near the plant,
pull up in a few days and you should see the wire-worms stick-
ing out of it, and you should know how to kill them.

What are known as fungus diseases are not usually much
trouble, but one can attack saxifragas. I once had a *S.aizoon*
variety sent me which developed red spots like measles; by
spraying several times with Cheshunt Compound I cured it.
Do this also to Kabschia saxifrages if you find rosettes dying off
mysteriously.

ENVOI

THIS is probably the last book I shall write on rock plants and it has been a pleasant bit of work to give you the results of what I have learnt in sixty years of rock gardening. I do not mean to suggest that I know everything, I am still learning and expect to do so until in a few years I pass into the Great Beyond.

You will find in catalogues plants I have not mentioned, either because they are very difficult or impossible in the open ground or so new and untried that it is wise to wait and see whether they are going to be good garden plants. If they are, the news soon gets round.

So here's luck to your small rock garden.

NURSERYMEN WHO SELL ROCK PLANTS

This is a list of those whose catalogues I receive regularly. There are, of course, others.

Boothman, Stuart, Nightingale Nursery, Maidenhead, Berks.

Davenport-Jones, H., Washfield Nursery, Hawkhurst, Kent.

Drake, Jack, Aviemore, Inverness-shire, Scotland.

Elliott, Joe, Broadwell Nursery, Moreton-in-Marsh, Glos.

Goodwin, A. R. & K. M., Stocklands, Long Bank, Bewdley, Worcs.

Hillier and Sons Ltd, Winchester, Hants.

Ingwersen, W. E. Th. Ltd, Birch Farm, Sharpthorne, East Grinstead, Sussex.

Kaye, Reginald, Waithman Nursery, Silverdale, Lancs.

Maryfield Nurseries, Leslie, Fife.

Moody, H. W., Longwood Nurseries, Bingley, Yorks.
Notcutt, R. C., Woodbridge, Suffolk.
Old Court Nurseries Ltd, Colwall, Malvern, Worcs.
Osmond, G., Wickwar, Glos.
Ponton, J. R., The Gardens, Kirknewton, Scotland.
Scott & Co. Ltd, Merriott, Somerset.
Shipton-on-Cherwell Nursery, Kidlington, Oxon.
Thacker, T., The Nurseries, Knowle, Warwickshire.
Waterperry Horticultural School, Wheatley, Oxon.

INDEX